DATE DUE			
OCT 3 = 72			
APR 1 4 1987			
JUL 1 4 1988			
~~NOV 0 6 1991~~			
1 3 1997			
MAR 2 9 1997			
MAR 1 7 1997			
APR 1 0 1997			
APR 1 0 1997			
GAYLORD 234			PRINTED IN U.S.A.

WHERE THEY GO IN WINTER

WHERE THEY GO IN WINTER

Written and illustrated by

MARGARET WARING BUCK

ABINGDON PRESS

Nashville   *New York*

FOR SUSAN

the little girl at the

Pequot-Sepos Wildlife Sanctuary

THIS BOOK is for young naturalists who are curious about the winter habits of North American wildlife. Each section of the manuscript was read and checked for accuracy by an authority on the subject.

The author wishes to express her thanks and appreciation to Ernest A. Lachner, Supervisor and Curator, Division of Fishes, and Karl V. Krombein, Chairman, Department of Entomology, Smithsonian Institution; William A. Lund, Assistant Professor of Zoology, University of Connecticut; Olin Sewall Pettingill, Jr., Director, Laboratory of Ornithology, Cornell University; Charles A. Reed, Professor, Department of Biological Sciences, College of Liberal Arts and Sciences, University of Illinois; Allen E. Greer, Research Assistant, Museum of Comparative Zoology, Harvard University.

CONTENTS

Books by Margaret Waring Buck

IN WOODS AND FIELDS

IN YARDS AND GARDENS

IN PONDS AND STREAMS

PETS FROM THE POND

SMALL PETS FROM WOODS AND FIELDS

ALONG THE SEASHORE

WHERE THEY GO IN WINTER

WHERE THEY GO IN WINTER

WHERE DO THEY GO?

When winter comes, what happens to all the wild creatures that we see in warm weather? Where are all the bugs, birds, and beasts?

In our temperate zone, where there are distinct seasons, we find a great change in the way that most creatures live during the warm and the cold times of the year.

In summer we have green plants and insects that eat them, birds that eat the insects, other kinds of animals that eat plants and smaller animals. We are surrounded by living things.

In winter plants die back to the roots or go to seed and most of the creatures that feed on them disappear. Snow falls on a quiet world. However, when spring comes, plant and animal life returns. Where have the various kinds of animals been throughout the winter?

This book tells about many of our common insects, fishes, amphibians, reptiles, birds, and mammals, and what they do in winter.

When we speak of the north, we mean the southern part of Canada and that part of the United States that has a cold winter season. Northern Canada and the Arctic region, we call the far north, and our southern states, the south.

Insects and Spiders

Insects go through several stages during their lives. Starting as eggs, they hatch into larvae, change into pupae, and finally transform into adults. (Some kinds skip the pupa stage.) All insects live through the winter in one, or sometimes two, of these stages.

Toward the end of summer and in autumn the insects start to prepare for cold weather. Some adults lay their eggs in the ground or in sturdy cases; some gather into large groups and get ready to migrate; others collect in sheltered places where they can hibernate. Some larvae crawl into holes in the ground, under the bark of trees, or similar places. Others change into pupae in the ground, inside hard skins, or in cocoons. Most kinds of insects become inactive when they are cold. Only a few kinds, like the beetles that live in icy caves and the snow fleas, are active in very low temperatures.

Spiders lay eggs that hatch into young which resemble the adults in shape if not in size or color. They do not have a larva or a pupa stage. Some kinds live through the winter as eggs inside a protective sac; others hibernate as young or as adult spiders.

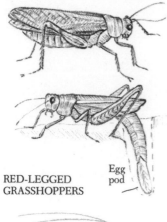

RED-LEGGED
GRASSHOPPERS

Egg
pod

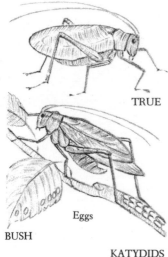

TRUE

Eggs

BUSH

KATYDIDS

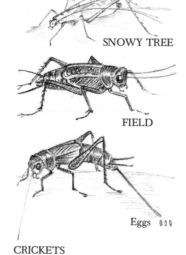

SNOWY TREE

FIELD

Eggs

CRICKETS

GRASSHOPPERS AND CRICKETS

Short-horned grasshoppers, or locusts, live through the winter as eggs or hibernate in the nymph form.

In fall the female RED-LEGGED GRASSHOPPER makes a hole in loose earth with her abdomen and lays a cluster of eggs in it. She coats the eggs with a gummy substance that hardens and forms a pod around them. This process may be repeated several times. In their protective pod the eggs survive the winter. When spring comes, the eggs break open and the larval grasshoppers (nymphs) push their way through the earth to the surface. They are shaped like the adults except that the abdomen is short and the wings have not developed. After growing and molting several times they become winged adults. The CAROLINA GRASSHOPPER also lays eggs that stay through the winter in the ground.

The NORTHERN GREEN-STRIPED GRASSHOPPER hibernates in deep grass in the nymph form. When the grass begins to grow in spring, the nymphs make their last molt and come out as adults. They are one of the first grasshoppers to appear in the spring.

Katydids are long-horned grasshoppers. They pass the winter as eggs. The TRUE KATYDID (the one that sings "katy-did") has broad wings that cover most of the body and look like green leaves. In autumn the female lays her eggs in slits in the bark of trees. The BUSH and ANGULAR-WINGED KATYDIDS have narrower wings. They lay their eggs in a row around the edge of a leaf or along a twig.

FIELD CRICKETS chirp day and night from spring through the last warm days of fall. When the weather grows cold, they creep into hiding places, but most of them die during the winter. Eggs laid in the ground by some species and hibernating nymphs of other species live through the winter.

SNOWY TREE CRICKETS sing in unison on warm nights in summer and early fall. Before cold weather comes, they lay their eggs in bark or plant stems. The adult crickets die in freezing weather, but the eggs live through the winter.

WALKING STICKS AND PRAYING MANTISES

WALKING STICKS are slender brown or green insects, three or four inches long. Except for some tropical species they do not have wings. In fact, they look so much like twigs on trees or bushes that they are seldom noticed. In autumn the females lay shiny eggs that are black with a white stripe and look like tiny beans. The eggs fall to the ground and lie there through the winter, long after all the stick insects have died. In the following, or sometimes the second, spring the eggs hatch into young that resemble the adults except in size and their paler color.

Praying mantises are large, voracious insects that catch smaller insects in their clawlike front legs. The CAROLINA MANTIS that lives in our eastern and southern states has a brownish or green body about 2½ inches long and green wings. It makes an oblong transparent but tough egg case on the branch of a tree.

The CHINESE PRAYING MANTIS, now common in the northeastern states, is brown with a green border on its long wings. In the fall when it is full grown, the female is 3½ inches or longer and the male a little smaller. After mating, the female is likely to consume the male before she sets out to find a place to make an egg case. After selecting a strong weed stem or branch of a shrub, she hangs on it head down. Then she squeezes a soft substance from the end of her body, whips it into a thick froth, and lays her eggs in it. The froth soon hardens into a tough case about the size and shape of a walnut. It remains on the stem to which it is attached throughout the winter and even after the eggs hatch in spring. The young mantises make a little ladder of holes along one side of the case when they emerge. You can tell that the case is old and empty if it feels soft and spongy and has a row of small holes. It is interesting to keep a Chinese mantis as a pet through the summer. It may be fed flies or other small insects and bits of raw beef from the end of a straw. But sometime in the fall it will die no matter how well fed and warm it is kept.

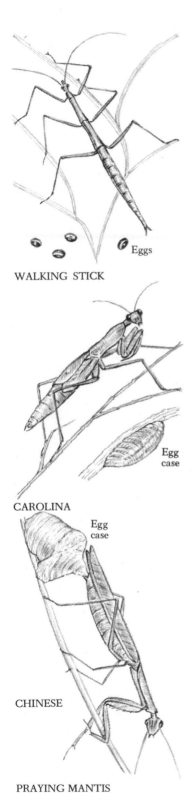

WALKING STICK

CAROLINA

CHINESE

PRAYING MANTIS

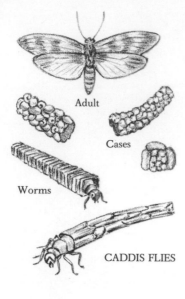

Adult

Cases

Worms

CADDIS FLIES

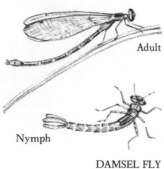

Adult

Nymph

DAMSEL FLY

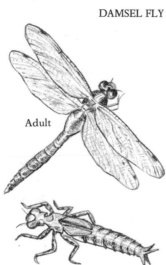

Adult

Nymph

DRAGONFLY

CADDIS AND DAMSEL FLIES, DRAGONFLIES

CADDIS FLIES resemble small moths. In summer they fly at night around lights and near water. They lay eggs on rocks or plants in the water. The eggs hatch into worms that live in the water and make cases from materials that they find there. Some kinds use pebbles; others use small shells or bits of plants. Most kinds form pupae inside their cases. Some spend the winter in the larval, some in the pupal, form. The following spring, summer, or fall they change into adults.

DAMSEL FLIES have long, slender bodies and gauzy wings. They fly in summer over ponds and fields. Sometimes the male and female fly together, and he is able to help pull her out of the water after she has laid her eggs. The larvae that hatch from the eggs are called nymphs. They live in the water and breathe through three flat gills at the tail end of the body. They feed on tiny water creatures. The nymphs live through the winter and remain active at least part of the time. In spring and summer they crawl out on land, split their skin, and change into the adult winged form.

DRAGONFLIES are sturdier than damsel flies. In fact, they are probably the strongest fliers among the insects. Some kinds of dragonflies migrate like birds. In the fall they gather into swarms and fly southward. They spend the winter in the southern states and return to the north in spring.

In summer dragonflies drop their eggs into the water of a pond or lay them in the leaves of submerged plants. The eggs hatch into hard-skinned nymphs that live on the bottom for a year or more. They feed on small water life, including tadpoles and young fishes, that they capture by thrusting out their lower jaw. The nymphs breathe oxygen from the water that passes in and out through the tail end. They can also shoot forward by squirting out the water.

In winter the nymphs hide under mud or rotting leaves in the water. In spring they resume activity. In summer those that are mature climb up plant stems into the air, split their skin down the back, and change into winged dragonflies.

WATER BUGS AND BEETLES

WATER STRIDERS, or SKATERS, are long-legged bugs that skim over the surface of ponds in summer. In cold weather they crawl under leaves or other shelter at the bottom or along the banks and hibernate. During a thaw they sometimes come out on the surface.

WATER BOATMEN and BACKSWIMMERS are small bugs that live in ponds and breathe air at the surface. Boatmen swim with their backs up, backswimmers with their backs down. Both live through the winter. In autumn they fly to ponds that contain water plants. In winter they are sometimes seen clinging to what is left of the plants or crowded into air pockets under the ice.

WATER SCORPIONS are insects that hang head down in the water with the long air tube at the tail end of their bodies thrust up to the surface. They also live among dead leaves and debris along the shore, and it is here that they spend the winter. One kind of scorpion, over two inches long, is slender and brown like a walking stick; the other, about one inch long, is broad, flat, and black.

WHIRLIGIG BEETLES are small black beetles, ¼ to ½ inch long, that whirl around on still water in summer. In very cold winter weather they are inactive, but on mild days they may be seen rotating in groups on the surface of open water.

WATER SCAVENGER BEETLES are black and from 1 to 1½ inches long. They swim underwater, carrying a film of air on the underside of their bodies. They eat small water life and decaying matter. Sometimes they are seen flying around lights. The beetles remain active through most of the winter.

DIVING BEETLES vary in length from ½ inch to over two inches. They often hang head down in the water with their tail ends sticking up for air. Before diving they collect an air bubble under their wings. In winter they may hibernate in mud at the pond bottom some of the time, but they are active at other times, especially as spring approaches. These beetles may live for several years.

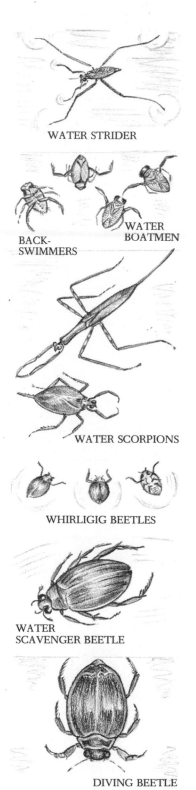

WATER STRIDER

BACK-SWIMMERS   WATER BOATMEN

WATER SCORPIONS

WHIRLIGIG BEETLES

WATER SCAVENGER BEETLE

DIVING BEETLE

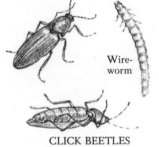

LADYBIRD BEETLES

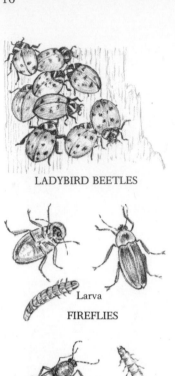

Larva

FIREFLIES

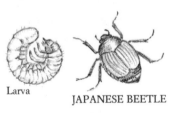

Wire-worm

CLICK BEETLES

Larva

JAPANESE BEETLE

Larva

MAY
BEETLE

BEETLES

LADYBIRD BEETLES are red or yellow with black spots, or black with red spots. Over a hundred different kinds are found in the United States. In warm weather both adult and larval beetles feed on aphids (plant lice). In the fall ladybirds collect in large numbers in certain favorite places. Along the west coast they may choose rocky crevices or open snowy places at the top of mountains. In the midwest and east they may collect under haystacks, fallen leaves, or logs — even in houses. In these places they hibernate.

Farmers and agricultural agents gather masses of hibernating beetles and keep them in cold storage until spring. Then they release the beetles on farm land to combat aphids.

At dusk in early summer FIREFLIES are seen flashing their tail lights over fields and lawns. Before they vanish in midsummer they lay eggs in rotting logs or fallen leaves. The eggs hatch into larvae that hibernate in their hatching places.

The larvae of CLICK BEETLES are long, thin worms with hard brown or yellow skins. They are called wireworms. Some kinds live in rotting wood; others live in the ground. Some live through several winters before they change into beetles. These beetles, when upside down, are able to bend their backs, snap into the air, and land right side up.

The grubs of JAPANESE BEETLES live in the ground under grass roots through the winter. In spring they pupate underground, and in summer the adult beetles emerge. Starlings help to control the beetles by digging with their bills around grass roots and eating the grubs.

The larvae of MAY BEETLES, or JUNE BUGS, are fat white grubs that live in the ground for two or three years. In winter they dig deeper and hibernate. In summer they eat grass and other plant roots. Late in summer those that are mature form pupae and change into adults. The adults hibernate underground until late spring. Then we see them around lights and hear them banging against windows. They lay eggs in the ground around grass roots and die soon after.

WASPS AND HORNETS

The PAPER WASP is the one that makes a nest of a single layer of cells that are open underneath. The nest hangs by a short stem from the eaves of a house or other support. A new nest is started every spring by a young queen wasp, since she is the only one to live through the winter. To make the paper for the nest she bites off bits of rotted wood, plant stems, or sometimes cardboard. These she chews up and mixes with saliva to form a pulp that hardens when it is dry. After making a few cells the queen lays eggs, one to a cell, and glues them in place. The larvae that hatch from the eggs hang head down and are fed from below. They develop into workers that will take care of the nest and young, freeing the queen of all duties but egg laying.

After midsummer males and females hatch from the eggs. In autumn the old queen, the workers, and the males die leaving only the females, who are now young queens. These seek shelter in buildings, logs, or other places, where they hibernate until spring. Then each one starts a new colony.

WHITE-FACED HORNETS live in an enclosed paper nest shaped like a football but a little larger in size. It hangs from a beam, branch, eaves, or other support. Although the queen hornet is the only one that lives through the winter, the colony that she starts in spring may number several thousand before the summer is over.

The queen makes the first paper cells of the nest and lays eggs in them. She feeds the larvae that hatch from the eggs until they develop into workers. The workers add to the nest and feed the new larvae. At the end of summer, males and females are raised. These mate, and the females become the young queens that will hibernate in logs, under fallen trees, or other shelter. In winter the large, sturdy hanging nest is deserted. Then it may be taken down and examined. If you cut one open, you will see that it contains several rows of combs with cells that are open on the underside. The thick outer wall is composed of many layers of paper.

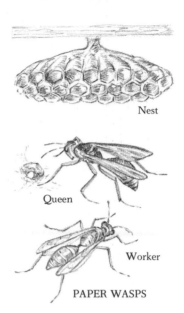

Nest

Queen

Worker

PAPER WASPS

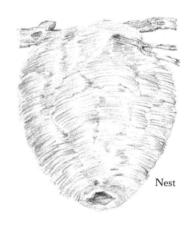

Nest

Drone

Queen

Worker

WHITE-FACED HORNETS

Queen

Drone

Worker

HONEYBEES

Male

Worker

Queen

BUMBLEBEES

BEES

Among the HONEYBEES it is the queen and the late summer brood of workers that live through the winter. In fall the workers collect sticky gum from buds and trees. This they use to seal cracks in the wall of the hive in order to make it tight. When cold weather comes, they stay inside. They do not raise any more young bees, since the queen stops laying eggs.

In very cold weather some of the bees crowd together near the center of the hive. They move their bodies and wings, and this releases heat. Other bees form an insulating layer around them. From time to time the bees change places. In this way they are able to keep the temperature of the hive much warmer than that of the air outside. To maintain this activity the bees must eat. They feed on the honey that they have stored in combs during the summer. People who raise bees and sell honey always leave enough in the hive for the bees to eat in winter.

At the end of winter the queen resumes her egg laying so that there will be some new workers when spring comes. Later, in the summer, if the hive becomes too crowded, the queen and some of the workers fly away to start a new colony.

In early summer the BUMBLEBEE colony consists of a queen and workers. Late in summer, male and female bees are raised. They mate, and the females become young queens. When cold weather comes, the workers, males, and the old queens die. Only the young queens live through the winter. Each one finds shelter in a hole in the ground, a hollow tree, or some other snug place where she can hibernate. Early in spring, when pussy willow and a few other plants are in bloom, the young queen awakens. At once she sets out to find a place for a nest such as a mousehole or a hollow under tree roots. In the hole she makes a honey pot and a cell out of wax from her body. She collects nectar from flowers for the honey pot and pollen for the cell where she will lay her first eggs. The eggs develop into workers that will enlarge the nest and take care of the next young.

BUTTERFLIES THAT MIGRATE

The MONARCH BUTTERFLY is the orange and black one seen in fields and gardens throughout the United States and much of Canada. It lays eggs on milkweed leaves. The eggs hatch into caterpillars that have yellow, black, and white stripes when they are full grown. They form pale green chrysalises that hang from leaves or other support for a week or two until the butterflies emerge. This process is repeated until the third set of butterflies appears at the end of summer. These late butterflies gather into groups and start southward. More join them along the way until the groups grow very large, often numbering in the thousands.

Monarchs from the eastern parts of Canada and the United States travel to Florida, the Gulf coast, and Mexico. Those from Alaska and the western coast go to California and Mexico. There are favorite places where the butterflies stay in winter and even favorite trees on which they rest.

At the approach of spring the butterflies start to straggle northward. They pause along the way to lay eggs. The butterflies which emerge on the way may be the ones that arrive in the north rather than those that went south in the fall.

The PAINTED LADY is reddish brown with black markings on the upper side. On the underside it has lacy white markings and a row of eyespots on the hind wing. It is found throughout North America, also in Europe and Africa. A strong flier, it has been seen at sea a long distance from land.

Although painted ladies may not migrate every year, large numbers of them travel occasionally. Swarms of southward flying butterflies have been seen in California in the fall, and larger swarms have been seen moving northward in spring. The butterflies apparently spend the winter in Mexico, where they raise another brood. On the northward journey one or two more broods may be raised. The black and yellow caterpillars feed on thistle, nettle, and other plants.

The butterflies that do not migrate probably hibernate in sheltered places.

MONARCH

PAINTED LADY

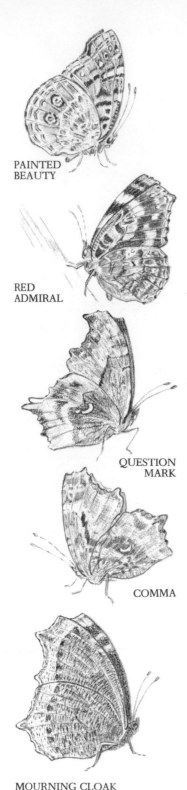

PAINTED
BEAUTY

RED
ADMIRAL

QUESTION
MARK

COMMA

MOURNING CLOAK

BUTTERFLIES THAT HIBERNATE

The PAINTED BEAUTY BUTTERFLY is much like the painted lady in color, golden brown and black on the upper wings; pink, brown, black, with white spots and veins on the under-wings. The caterpillar is black with light lines and is spiny. It lives on white everlasting flowers and leaves and makes its hanging chrysalis there. A chrysalis that is made in late summer may remain through the winter, but usually the butterfly emerges, finds a sheltered spot, and hibernates.

The RED ADMIRAL, a brown and black butterfly with orange bands and white spots on its upper wings, is found throughout the northern hemisphere. Its caterpillar feeds on nettles. Of its late summer brood, some remain in the chrysalis through the winter, some hibernate as butterflies, and a few may migrate. Newly emerged butterflies are in perfect shape in spring, but the ones that hibernated are apt to be tattered.

QUESTION-MARK BUTTERFLIES have a violet tinge over their reddish-brown wings especially noticeable on the tip of the hind wing. They are found over most of the United States. The caterpillars feed on nettle, elm, and hops. There are two summer broods of butterflies. The second one hibernates under loose bark, in hollow logs, or other shelter.

The COMMA BUTTERFLY, named from the silver comma-shaped mark on the underside of the hind wings, is related to and has the same habits as the question-mark.

The MOURNING CLOAK BUTTERFLY, velvety brown with a yellow border on its wings, is found throughout the northern hemisphere. Its caterpillar feeds on poplar, willow, and elm and is sometimes called the spiny elm caterpillar. In the north it has only one brood a year, and the butterflies live from one summer until the next. Sometimes they have a rest period in summer as well as through the winter. They hibernate in hollow trees, under eaves, or in buildings. Early in spring they come out and may be found around houses and gardens. When caught and held in the hand they have a curious habit of playing dead.

BUTTERFLY CATERPILLARS AND CHRYSALISES

The butterflies on this page pass the winter in the larva (caterpillar) or the chrysalis (pupa) stage.

In early autumn the GREAT SPANGLED FRITILLARY lays its eggs on or near violet plants. The eggs soon hatch into caterpillars that eat nothing but their eggshells. Then they find hiding places and hibernate. In spring they awaken and feed at night on violet leaves. When the caterpillars are full grown, they form chrysalises and transform into butterflies that are brown and black with silver spots underneath.

Caterpillars of the bark-colored WOOD NYMPH and related butterflies are green like the grass on which they feed. Soon after they hatch in midsummer, they go into hibernation.

The SILVER-SPOTTED SKIPPER caterpillar feeds on locust leaves. It makes a shelter in the leaves by fastening two together with silk. When it is ready to change, it forms a pupa in the leaves or in a loosely spun cocoon on the ground. Some other kinds of skipper caterpillars line oak or willow leaves with silk and hibernate there.

The VICEROY caterpillar eats the leaves of willow, poplar, and aspen trees. Before cold weather comes, it makes a silken nest in a rolled up leaf that it fastens with silk to a branch. Inside the nest it hibernates.

The BLACK SWALLOWTAIL caterpillar eats the leaves of carrot, parsley, and related plants. When full grown it forms a chrysalis and transforms. A second brood, later in summer, does not transform. The chrysalis hangs through the winter and changes into a butterfly the following May or June.

The green TIGER SWALLOWTAIL caterpillar is broad at the head end, where it has two large eyespots. It feeds on the leaves of wild cherry, birch, apple, and other trees. Chrysalises formed by the second brood live through the winter.

The white CABBAGE BUTTERFLY has three broods of small green caterpillars that feed on cabbage leaves. The last brood lives through the winter in the form of chrysalises fastened to branches, boards, or other support.

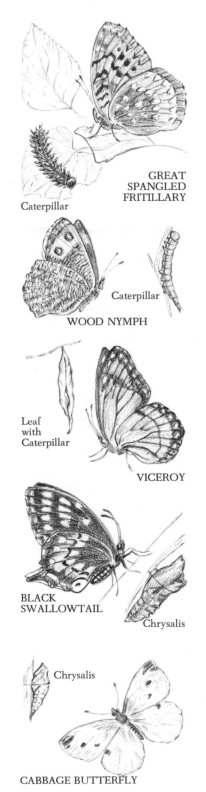

GREAT SPANGLED FRITILLARY

Caterpillar

Caterpillar

WOOD NYMPH

Leaf with Caterpillar

VICEROY

BLACK SWALLOWTAIL

Chrysalis

Chrysalis

CABBAGE BUTTERFLY

PROMETHEA — Cocoon

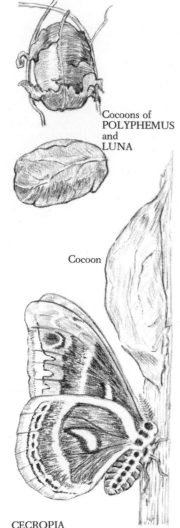

Cocoons of
POLYPHEMUS
and
LUNA

Cocoon

CECROPIA

MOTH COCOONS

Although all caterpillars can spin silk, butterfly caterpillars do not use it to make cocoons. The caterpillars, or silkworms, of the large night-flying moths make the big cocoons that we find in winter on the branches of trees, shrubs, and weeds in the eastern half of the United States.

The PROMETHEA caterpillar is green and about two inches long. In the fall it makes a slender cocoon inside a hanging leaf. After fastening the stem to a branch, it lines the leaf with silk, draws the edges together, and forms a pupa inside. The cocoon hangs until late in the following spring. Then the moth emerges. Its wingspread is about four inches and the color is shades of reddish brown with a tan border.

The POLYPHEMUS caterpillar is green with orange spots on the sides and about three inches long. It also makes a cocoon inside a hanging leaf, but its cocoon is fatter than that of the promethea. Late in spring a very large moth emerges from the cocoon. It has tan wings with yellow borders, and each hind wing has a large eyespot.

The LUNA caterpillar, about three inches long, is green with a yellow line and red spots along the sides. The cocoon that it makes between leaves falls to the ground, where it stays until June or later in the following year. Then a beautiful moth with pale green wings emerges.

The CECROPIA caterpillar, found on cherry, maple, and other trees, grows to be four inches long. It is bluish green with blue, black, yellow, and red tubercles on its back. It makes one of the largest and most easily found of the cocoons. Fastened lengthwise to a branch, the cocoon has a tough parchment-like covering that protects the pupa inside throughout the winter. Early in the following summer the pupa transforms into a very large moth with richly colored wings in shades of reddish brown marked with white and black.

Caterpillar

MOTH CATERPILLARS AND PUPAE

The caterpillar of the ISABELLA TIGER MOTH is the brown and black WOOLLY BEAR that we see crawling along roadsides in the fall. It is looking for a spot under leaves or other shelter where it can curl up and hibernate. It does not make a cocoon until spring. Then it forms a soft, rounded one with hairs from its body worked into the silk. The cocoon lies on the ground for a month or so until the pupa inside is ready to transform into a yellowish-tan medium-sized moth.

Cocoon

WOOLLY
BEAR

The caterpillars of the hawk, or sphinx, moths are smooth. Because of the small horn at the end of the body, they are called hornworms. Their habit of raising the front part of the body and drawing the head in gives them a sphinx-like appearance. Most of them do not make cocoons. In late summer or fall they wriggle into the ground and form hard-shelled pupae. These stay in the ground until spring. Then they work up to the surface by boring with the point of their abdomen. They transform into stout-bodied, narrow-winged moths.

ISABELLA TIGER

One kind of hawk moth caterpillar is the large green or brown worm found on tomato plants. It forms a brown pupa with a little handle at the head end which encases the tongue of the developing moth. The moth, called the TOMATO SPHINX, has variegated brown wings and orange spots on the abdomen. Its long tongue, coiled when not in use, enables it to sip nectar from flowers.

STRIPED
SPHINX

The STRIPED SPHINX MOTH has brown and white forewings and a pink band on the hind wings. Its caterpillar, three inches long, varies in color from yellowish green with red, yellow, and black spots to black with a line and spots of yellow. The caterpillar sometimes makes a loose cocoon among fallen leaves; more often it forms a two-inch-long tan pupa in the ground.

Caterpillar

Pupa

TOMATO SPHINX

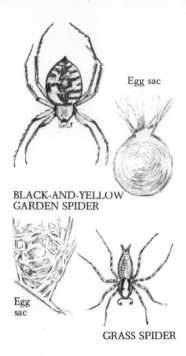

BLACK-AND-YELLOW
GARDEN SPIDER

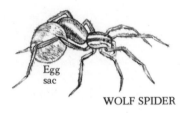

Egg
sac

GRASS SPIDER

Egg
sac

WOLF SPIDER

CRAB SPIDERS

DADDY LONGLEGS

SPIDERS

BLACK-AND-YELLOW GARDEN SPIDERS spin the large webs that we see in summer stretched between plant stalks or shrubs. By the end of summer these spiders are full grown, the females about an inch long in the body, the males much smaller. After mating, the female leaves her web and seeks a sheltered spot under twigs, bark, or boards. Here she spins a tiny silken sac and crowds her many eggs into it. A thick matted layer is around the eggs and a tough parchment-like coat over it. So the egg sac is well protected from the cold weather that will soon take the spider's life.

Soon the young spiders hatch. They eat their eggshells, and some eat other spiders. The ones that are left hibernate in the sac until the following spring.

GRASS SPIDERS make flat or funnel-shaped webs that catch drops of dew or rain. In autumn the female makes an egg sac on stems or twigs near the ground. Over it she spins a loose web in which bits of earth and twigs are caught. This protects the egg sac until the following spring, when the young spiders are ready to emerge.

WOLF SPIDERS do not make real webs. Some kinds live in silk-lined holes in the ground. In the fall the female makes a small ball-shaped egg sac that remains attached to the end of her body until the young hatch. The young cling to the mother's back for a short time. Then they drop off and roam until cold weather comes, when they hibernate.

Some kinds of CRAB SPIDERS live on fences and buildings; others live on flowers. They do not spin webs. In cold weather these spiders hide in cracks in walls or other sheltered places. They may come out on sunny days.

DADDY LONGLEGS, or HARVESTMEN, are related to spiders, but they do not have silk glands for making webs. They travel over plants on their long legs. In autumn the females lay their eggs in the ground or in cracks in wood. The adults of most species die in cold weather, but the eggs survive and hatch the following spring.

Fishes

Where fishes go in winter depends partly upon whether they like warm or cold water. The body temperature of most fishes is the same as that of the water in which they live, and they cannot stand sudden drastic changes. Some fishes like cold water. They live in it and remain active throughout the year. Some of the fishes that prefer warm water go deeper in winter, since the temperature near the bottom is not as low as it is near the surface. Some of the ocean fishes migrate to warmer southern waters.

Some kinds of fishes travel in winter in order to find more food. Other kinds, which breed at this time, travel in order to find the right sort of place to lay their eggs.

Fishes that live in lakes and ponds may not do much traveling. When the water becomes cold and the food supply diminishes, some of them move to the bottom and become dormant in the mud. While dormant they do not need as much oxygen, but they do need some. In a shallow pond that is covered with ice and snow the supply of oxygen may give out. If this happens, the fishes will die. That is why dead fishes are sometimes found floating on a pond after the ice melts.

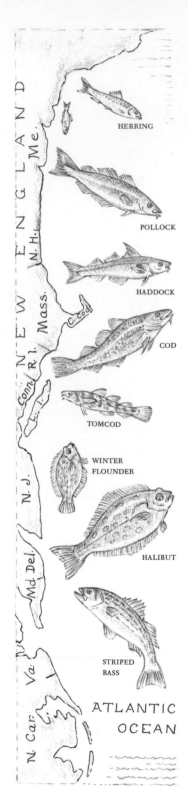

IN THE NORTHERN ATLANTIC

The fishes on this page live in cool salt water. They are found in winter off our northern Atlantic coast.

HERRING move inshore to spawn in the fall. In winter they swim in huge schools off the New England coast, where they feed on plankton and small crustaceans. The young fish remain near the shore. Many are caught in weirs by commercial fisheries, put in cans, and labeled sardines.

POLLOCK spawn in fall and winter near the New England coast. The young fish stay near the shore. Older fish move into deeper water and in summer go farther north. They feed on small fishes and shrimp.

COD roam in schools over the sea bottom, where they feed on mollusks, crustaceans, starfish, and small fishes. They spawn in winter and early spring off the New England coast.

TOMCOD, also called frostfish, are small codfish that swim off the New England coast and feed on small crustaceans and fishes. They spawn in winter at the mouths of rivers.

HADDOCK live at the bottom in deep water, where they feed on invertebrates. The young hatch in late spring and float near the surface for three months before sinking down.

WINTER FLOUNDERS live in shallow bays in winter. They stay on the bottom and feed on crustaceans, mollusks, and small fishes. They spawn in brackish water and offshore in winter and early spring. In summer they go into deeper water.

SUMMER FLOUNDERS go into deeper water in winter and spawn well offshore. In summer they go into shallow water along the New England coast.

The HALIBUT is a large flounder found in northern but not very cold water. It lives on the bottom from several hundred to several thousand feet down. The largest halibut live in the deepest water.

STRIPED BASS live along the mid-Atlantic coast in winter. They usually stay near the shore, where they feed on smaller fishes, crustaceans, and worms. In spring they move northward and go up rivers to spawn.

FROM NORTHERN ATLANTIC SOUTHWARD

The fishes on this page prefer fairly warm salt water. In winter they travel southward or into deeper water along our Atlantic coast.

BLACKFISH, or TAUTOG, live in shallow water along our northeastern coast in summer. They feed around rocks and piers on mollusks that they crush with their teeth. In the fall some move south to the Carolinas; others go into deeper water.

CUNNERS are often found with the blackfish to which they are related. They live off the Canadian and New England coasts throughout the year. A very severe winter may kill large numbers of both cunners and blackfish.

MACKEREL swim in huge schools between Labrador and Cape Hatteras. In summer they are found in northern coastal waters, where they feed near the surface on plankton. In the fall they move southward and into deeper water. In the winter they sink lower and may become less active.

Large schools of PORGY, or SCUP, appear off the New England coast in summer. They feed on the bottom on squids, mollusks, and small fishes. In cold weather they migrate to deeper water off the Virginia capes.

BUTTERFISH swim in schools over sandy bottoms near our northern shores in summer. In winter they are found in deep water south to Florida.

KINGFISH also swim in schools over sand along the New England coast in summer, where they feed on squid, crustaceans, mollusks, and young fishes. In winter they migrate to warmer water. Some live off the Carolina coast all the year.

WEAKFISH are found off New England in summer, in southern waters throughout the year. They feed on small fishes and invertebrates found in surf and swift channels.

BLUEFISH are found off our southern coast throughout the year and off the northeastern coast in spring, summer, and fall. In winter the northern bluefish may move offshore into deeper water. Young bluefish, called snappers, are caught by fishermen from the shore, piers, and bridges.

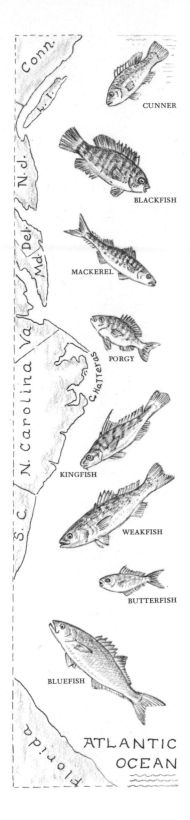

CUNNER

BLACKFISH

MACKEREL

PORGY

KINGFISH

WEAKFISH

BUTTERFISH

BLUEFISH

ATLANTIC OCEAN

SHAD

ALEWIFE

SMELT

PACIFIC SALMON

THAT GO UPSTREAM TO SPAWN

Fishes lay eggs (spawn) that hatch into tiny tadpole-shaped larvae or fry. The fry feed on minute water life as they grow and develop. After a few weeks they usually have the shape though not the size of the adult. The fry are often able to feed and develop better in shallow water. Many fishes lay their eggs in marshes, ponds, and the edge of lakes. Some kinds of saltwater fishes leave the sea at spawning time and go up freshwater streams.

SHAD live in the sea, where they swim in huge schools and feed on plankton. At three or more years of age they move toward the coast in winter and spring. When the water in coastal rivers starts to get warm, the shad ascend to their spawning places. Some males go first; others follow with the females. Each female lays her thousands of eggs in shallow water over a sandy or pebbly bottom. In about a week the eggs hatch, but the young fish wait until fall before they swim out to sea. Adult shad return to the sea in summer.

The habits of the ALEWIFE are similar to those of the shad, whom they precede up coastal rivers at spawning time.

SMELT swim in large schools in cool water off the Atlantic coast. In fall they enter tidal bays and stay there through the winter. In spring they go up streams to spawn. In shallow riffles the females lay sticky eggs that adhere to the bottom. Some adults die after spawning, but most return to the sea. Smelt also live in lakes in the Great Lakes area, where some are caught in winter by fishermen through holes in the ice.

Along the coast from California to Alaska there are five kinds of PACIFIC SALMON. They live in the sea from two to six years then go up rivers to spawn. Some of them travel for hundreds of miles over a period of several months, during which time they do not feed. After spawning they are worn out and die. The eggs are laid in late summer or fall in gravel nests, where they stay until the following spring before hatching. Some of the young fish stay in fresh water for a year or two before heading for the sea; other kinds start at once.

ATLANTIC SALMON live in the sea from two to four years. Then, in the spring, they start up rivers, traveling toward the places where they were hatched. By the fall they have reached their destinations and are ready to spawn. The females make nests and lay their eggs in gravel at the bottom of fairly shallow water. The eggs remain in the nests through the winter and hatch the following spring. After spawning, the adult salmon return to the sea. The young salmon remain in fresh water about two years before they journey to the sea.

In some of our northern lakes Atlantic salmon remain throughout their lives. These fish do not grow as large as those that go to sea.

ATLANTIC SALMON

AMERICAN EEL

THAT GO TO SEA TO SPAWN

The AMERICAN EEL lives most of its life in fresh water and goes to sea to spawn. For six, seven, or more years the eels live in lakes and rivers, the males in brackish water near the river mouth and the females farther inland. During this time the eels are dormant in winter, buried in mud. In warm weather they resume activity and growth. The females grow to a length of four or five feet and the males to 2½ or three feet. In the autumn of the year that they are full grown and mature, the eels stop eating and their skin turns silvery.

Then they head for the sea and travel southward in the Atlantic until they come to deep water south of Bermuda in the seaweed-filled Sargasso Sea. Here each female lays her millions of tiny eggs. This large number is needed because the larvae that hatch from the eggs have to travel back to the Atlantic coast, and many perish on the way. Since the adult eels die after spawning, the larvae are needed to replace them.

It takes the small, transparent, leaf-shaped larvae about a year to reach the coast. Then they are about three inches long. They change their shape and color to become small eels, or elvers. In spring the elvers start up coastal rivers, growing bigger along the way. Some go far inland and may even travel over land in wet weather to reach lakes.

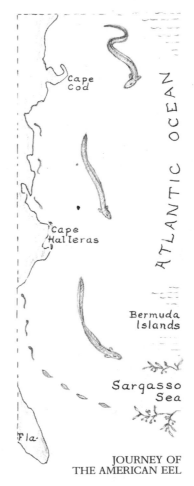

JOURNEY OF
THE AMERICAN EEL

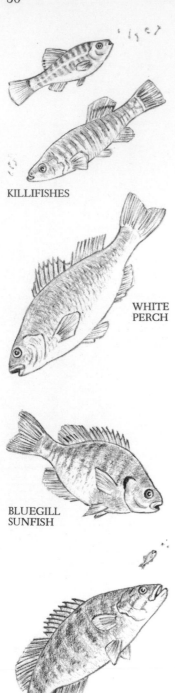

KILLIFISHES

WHITE
PERCH

BLUEGILL
SUNFISH

SMALLMOUTHED
BASS

DORMANT IN FRESH OR BRACKISH WATER

KILLIFISHES are small minnow-like fish that live in ponds, streams, and salt marshes, often in shallow, weed-filled water near the shore. They are greenish on the back with dark bars on the sides and yellowish underneath. Very hardy, they are able to stand changes in temperature and salinity and to live in water in which many other fishes could not survive. In winter killifishes may go into deeper water or remain dormant in marshes.

The WHITE PERCH, a favorite of fishermen, lives in ponds, creeks, and bays along the Atlantic coast. In winter the perch congregate in deeper water and remain there in a sluggish or a dormant state.

DORMANT IN FRESH WATER

SUNFISHES are brightly colored, medium-sized fishes. One kind or several kinds may be found in most ponds and lakes throughout the country. Easy to catch, they are popular with fishermen of all ages. In winter they are inactive, but some, like the bluegill, may take bait when it is dropped through a hole in an ice-covered pond.

Fishermen catch BASS in lakes, ponds, and streams in most parts of the United States. The smallmouth kind weighs up to six pounds, the largemouth to over eight pounds, and the spotted kind is in between. Bass grow larger in the southern part of their range, where they feed throughout the year. In the north they feed less in autumn, and in winter they may not feed at all. Then they usually retire to deeper water and remain dormant on the bottom, where they may take shelter under rocks or logs.

BULLHEADS, or HORNED POUTS, are smallish, dark-colored catfishes. They grow to about a foot in length and two pounds in weight. They are used as food, although they sometimes have a muddy flavor. With the barbels around their mouths they feel along the bottom searching for the plants and small water creatures that they eat. They live in ponds and slow streams, sometimes in shallow, weed-filled water. They can get along with less oxygen in the water than most fishes. They can even live out of water for a time if their gills and skin are kept moist.

In the late fall bullheads become sluggish and stop feeding. They may bury themselves in the bottom mud or under fallen leaves in shallow water near the shore. During the winter they remain dormant. Sometimes the ponds in which they stay are frozen almost solid; yet some of them survive.

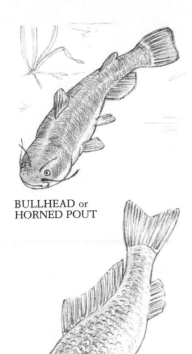

BULLHEAD or
HORNED POUT

CARP are large members of the minnow family. They grow to a length of three feet and a weight of twenty pounds. In color they vary from dark greenish brown to golden red or silvery. They live on the bottom of ponds and lakes, where they poke around in the mud to find the small animals, plants, and roots that they eat. In fall they usually feed well and put on a layer of body fat. In winter they may wriggle into the bottom mud until their bodies are nearly covered. During the coldest weather they lie in a deep sleep. Their breathing slows down, and they appear to be dead. But during a warm spell they slowly revive and in spring they are active again. Then they go into the shallow water of bays or the headwaters of streams in order to spawn.

CARP

GOLDFISH are relatives of the carp. The ones that live in ponds in a wild state grow fairly large and become darker in color. Like the carp (and many others), they put on a layer of fat in the summer or fall. This sustains them during the winter while they hibernate at the bottom of the pond. They can survive in an ice-covered pond as long as the water is not solidly frozen. Both carp and goldfish have been found alive although encased in ice. As long as their bodies are not frozen through, they are able to live, at least for a time.

Soon after the goldfish come out of hibernation, they are ready for spawning. Then they seek shallow places where there are water plants. An outdoor pool for goldfish should have a shallow place for spawning and a place at least three feet deep to provide protection from extreme heat or cold.

GOLDFISH

BROOK
TROUT

YELLOW
PERCH

NORTHERN
PIKE

CHAIN PICKEREL

ACTIVE IN FRESH WATER

BROOK TROUT are found in cool, swift-flowing streams in the United States and Canada. In large streams they may grow to a length of eighteen inches and a weight of several pounds. In small brooks they grow only six to eight inches long. On the back they are dark with light markings; on the sides they have red spots.

Brook trout move up small creeks to spawn in shallow places in the fall. The females make nests in the bottom gravel and lay their eggs. The eggs remain there all winter and do not hatch until the water warms up in spring.

YELLOW PERCH live in lakes and rivers in Canada and the United States. They are olive on the back, yellow with dark bars on the sides, and white underneath. From ten to fourteen inches long and a pound or more in weight, they are good pan fish. Active throughout the year, perch feed on small fishes, insects, and crustaceans. In late winter and early spring they spawn in weedy shallows along pond and lake shores. The female lays her many eggs in a band of jelly that is folded up like an accordion. Pulled out, it may be several feet long.

The NORTHERN PIKE is a long-bodied fish that grows to a length of three or four feet. It is a prized catch of fishermen throughout the year. In winter they sometimes spear it through the ice. The pike is bluish or greenish gray on the back, and it has lighter spots on the sides. It lives in lakes and streams in our northern states and Canada. A lone hunter and a voracious feeder, it captures smaller fishes and is active all year. It may spend the early part of the winter in deep water and later move into shallow water. As soon as the ice breaks in the spring, the pike go upstream or to the edge of lakes to find spawning places in shallow, weed-filled water.

The CHAIN PICKEREL lives in shallow lakes, ponds, or streams, where it lurks among water weeds and preys on minnows or other small water creatures. It is active all winter. In spring it follows the pike upstream into shallow places, where it will spawn.

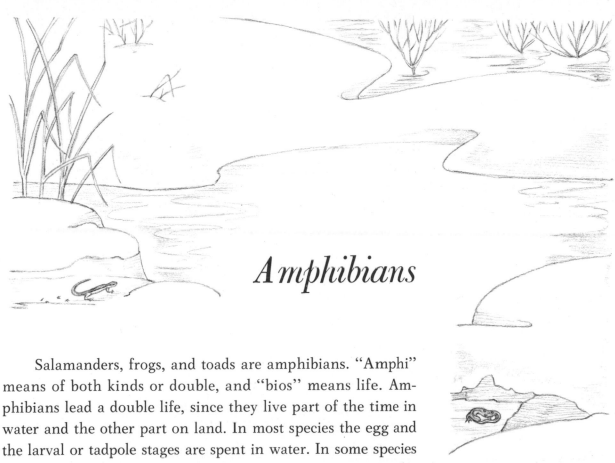

Amphibians

Salamanders, frogs, and toads are amphibians. "Amphi" means of both kinds or double, and "bios" means life. Amphibians lead a double life, since they live part of the time in water and the other part on land. In most species the egg and the larval or tadpole stages are spent in water. In some species the adult stage is spent on land; in some it is spent in the water; others live on land and in the water.

Amphibians have a moist skin that is smooth, rough, or granular, but almost never scaly. They are cold-blooded and so have about the same temperature as their surroundings. They are not able to stand extreme heat or cold. In summer they seek cool, moist places. In winter they hibernate under shelter on the ground, underground, or underwater. During hibernation their body processes, including breathing, slow down. They need only a little oxygen. Those that hibernate in mud or bottom debris underwater are able to absorb enough oxygen through their skin to supply their needs. For those that hibernate underground the oxygen that penetrates the soil is sufficient. Nourishment is furnished by the absorption of their body fat.

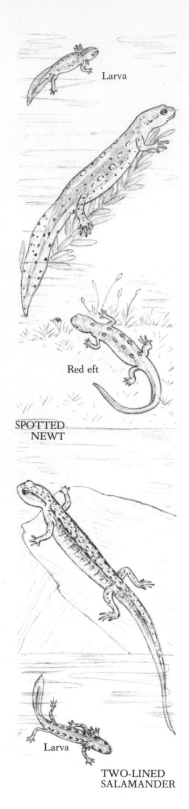

Larva

Red eft

SPOTTED
NEWT

Larva

TWO-LINED
SALAMANDER

SPOTTED NEWTS AND SALAMANDERS

The SPOTTED NEWT, about four inches long, is olive green with red and black spots on the back and yellow underneath. It is common in or beside quiet fresh water in the eastern and central states and into Canada. The female newt lays jelly-coated eggs on water plants in spring. The larvae that hatch in a few weeks live in water until the end of summer. Then, except in a few localities, they change into red efts that will live in the woods from one to three years. In summer the efts crawl among fallen leaves, looking for insects and worms to eat. In winter they hibernate under forest debris. When ready to transform into newts, usually in fall, they enter ponds.

In fall and early winter newts are active around water plants or at the bottom of ponds where they are able to find insects, worms, and crustaceans to eat. Later they may hibernate in the bottom mud or under moss on the bank.

The three following salamanders live in or near brooks and streams in the eastern part of the United States. In winter they usually stay in running water. They are active in mild weather, feeding on insects, worms, and small crustaceans. In very cold weather they usually seek shelter at the bottom, where they crawl under stones or debris.

The TWO-LINED SALAMANDER grows three or four inches long. In spring or summer the female lays eggs in small blobs of jelly under rocks in the water. The larvae live in water for two or three years before changing into the adult form.

The adult RED SALAMANDER may be six inches long. In fall the female lays her eggs under stones in water. The larvae hatch late in the fall but are not active until spring. They live in water for two and a half years before transforming.

The DUSKY SALAMANDER grows four or five inches long, the female being smaller than the male. She lays her eggs in summer in a moist place on the ground. She guards them until they hatch in about two months. The larvae soon find their way to water, where they stay until they transform the following spring.

SALAMANDERS

The two species that follow live in the woods in the eastern states. The RED-BACKED SALAMANDER grows about five inches long. In summer the female lays jelly-coated eggs in rotting logs or under moist wood. She guards the eggs, and in the fall they hatch into larvae that are able to live on land. Most of the gill-bearing stage is passed in the egg. In cold weather these salamanders go underground to a depth of from several inches to more than a foot. Those that do not go deep enough may not survive.

The FOUR-TOED SALAMANDER is a small one that has four instead of five toes on its hind feet. In spring the female lays eggs under moss on the ground near water. The larvae wriggle to the water and live there until they transform from midsummer to early fall. In winter these salamanders hibernate in groups in logs, under leaves, or in holes in the ground.

The four following species are called MOLE SALAMANDERS. They are large (from five to eight inches long), stout-bodied creatures found on moist land in most of the United States and into Canada. During the day they hide under earth or debris. At night they hunt for worms, snails, and insects to eat. Those that live in cold places hibernate under earth, piles of leaves, logs, or other shelter. Some, especially the spotted ones, may get into cellars or window wells.

Early in spring the females of the SPOTTED, JEFFERSON'S, and TIGER SALAMANDERS lay their eggs in jelly-coated masses in ponds. After a few weeks the eggs hatch into larvae that live in water until the middle or end of summer. Then they change to the adult form and take to the woods. (In the southwestern states adult tiger salamanders may be water creatures.)

MARBLED SALAMANDERS live in drier places than the others. They lay their eggs in autumn instead of spring and on the ground near water, usually in a low place that will be flooded by rain. When that happens, the larvae hatch and wriggle or float to the water. If the autumn is dry, the eggs may not hatch until the spring rains come.

MARBLED

TIGER

SPOTTED

MOLE SALAMANDERS

GREEN FROG

FROGS

GREEN FROGS live in or at the edge of ponds in the eastern part of the United States and Canada. Their color varies, but they are usually bright green around the head, brownish with black spots on the back, and light underneath; the male has a yellow throat. A fold of skin along each side of the back as well as their smaller size distinguishes them from bullfrogs. They grow 3½ or four inches long, the female being larger.

Green frogs are active in spring, but they do not mate and lay eggs until early summer. The jelly-coated eggs lie in flat masses at the surface of shallow or weedy water. They soon hatch into tadpoles that grow throughout the summer, but do not change into frogs until the following year.

In winter the tadpoles burrow into mud and remain at the bottom of the pond. The frogs hibernate in the bottom mud, under stones in springs, in burrows in the banks of the pond, and under moist leaves.

BULLFROGS live in ponds and lakes in most of eastern United States and Canada. They are greenish brown on the back, white with dark markings underneath, and the male has a yellow throat. He grows to 7½ inches in length, the female to eight inches. Bullfrogs do not collect in large numbers in one place even at breeding time, when we hear only one or two croaking in a pond. This occurs in late spring in the south, in early summer in the north.

The female lays her eggs in jelly-covered masses that may measure two feet across. The masses float on the surface, usually anchored by stems of water plants. The tadpoles grow for two years or more until they are over five inches long before they are ready to change into frogs. In the south they may remain active in the water all winter. In the north they stay near the bottom on cool days in the fall, swim on

BULLFROG   Tadpole

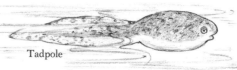

sunny days, then finally dig into the bottom mud and hibernate through the cold weather.

The frogs also hibernate under mud and bottom debris in the water. In cold climates this may be from early fall until May or June.

The LEOPARD FROG is a handsome, smooth-skinned frog that is found in ponds or meadows in most of the United States, Southern Canada, Mexico, and into Central America. It grows three or four inches long and is green or brownish with dark spots that are rimmed with white. In spring these frogs collect in ponds, pools, or marshes, where they mate and lay masses of jelly-coated eggs. The eggs hatch into tadpoles that are ready to change into frogs by the end of summer.

During the summer the adult frogs live on land, but in the fall they head for a pond or brook. They swim about for a while, near the surface in warmer weather, deeper in cooler weather. When cold weather comes to stay, they go to the bottom and sink into the mud or crawl under a rock with their heads down and legs spread out. They can withstand low temperatures and live after being encased in ice if their bodies are not frozen through, and they thaw out gradually.

The PICKEREL FROG is a little smaller than the leopard frog and is more brownish in color. The dark spots on its back are not outlined in white, and it has a wash of orange under its hind legs that is lacking in the leopard frog. It has an odorous skin secretion that is poisonous to other animals.

Pickerel frogs are found in the same general area as leopard frogs. In spring large numbers of them collect in the shallow water of ponds to mate and lay eggs. After a week or two the eggs hatch into tadpoles that will change into frogs in late summer.

During the summer pickerel frogs may live on moist land, but when fall comes they return to the water. They enter marshes, ponds, springs, or brooks. In the cold part of their range they may hibernate from September or October until late March or April.

Young frog

LEOPARD FROG

Young frog

PICKEREL FROG

SPRING
PEEPER

EASTERN
TREE FROG

WOOD
FROG

AMERICAN TOAD

FROGS AND TOADS

The SPRING PEEPER, found in the eastern states and Canada, is heard peeping in ponds in early spring. After laying its eggs it returns to the land, where it lives among grasses and shrubs throughout the summer. Around the middle of October it usually burrows into soft ground that is covered with leaves or moss. Here it stays until February or March. Some peepers have been found in springs in winter.

The EASTERN TREE FROG, or TOAD, lays its eggs in swamps and ponds in spring. In summer it lives in a tree, where it may be heard trilling in the evening or on cloudy days. In fall, before the first frost, it burrows under tree roots or goes into a rotting log and sleeps through the winter. In the warmer parts of its range it may remain active.

The WOOD FROG of the eastern states and Canada is brown like the fallen leaves of the forest floor, where it lives most of the year. In spring it is one of the first to enter a pond to lay its eggs. Sometimes the eggs are laid in shallow water so early that they freeze.

Around the end of September the wood frog crawls under a stone, log, or dead leaves on the ground in the forest. There it flattens out and sleeps until March or April. In the southern part of its range it may not hibernate as long.

The warty-skinned AMERICAN TOAD is common throughout eastern North America. In spring it enters a pond and lays its eggs in long strings of jelly. The tiny black tadpoles that hatch from the eggs change into small toads early in summer. During summer we often find toads in gardens.

In a cold climate the toad is usually ready to retire in September. It finds a slightly moist place like the bank of a pond, the ground under a stone foundation, or soft garden soil. There it works its body backward into the ground and, as the weather grows colder, it digs deeper until it is below the frost line. It remains dormant until spring. In a warm place like a greenhouse the toad does not hibernate, but it eats less and sleeps more than usual.

Reptiles

Snakes and turtles are reptiles. The name reptile comes from a Latin word meaning to creep. Snakes creep on their bellies; turtles crawl on short legs. Reptiles are covered with scales or horny plates. Some kinds live in dry places; others live in or near water; but they all lay their eggs on land. Even pond turtles lay their eggs in holes in the earth or in sand. Turtle eggs, laid in spring or summer, usually hatch before cold weather. But some do not hatch until the following spring. They survive the winter buried below the frost line.

Egg-laying snakes deposit their eggs in places where there are piles of decaying leaves or rotting wood. Some snakes bear their young alive. Young snakes and turtles resemble their parents; they do not have a larval stage.

Like amphibians, reptiles are cold-blooded. Their temperature changes with that of their surroundings. They are not able to remain long in a very hot or a very cold place. On hot summer days they seek shady spots. At the beginning of cold weather they look for sheltered places that the frost cannot reach. There they remain throughout the winter in a deep sleep.

GARTER SNAKE

WATER SNAKE

MILK SNAKE

COPPERHEAD

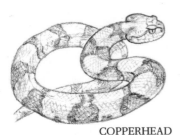

RATTLESNAKE

SNAKES

During warm weather snakes live in fields or woods with the exception of the water snakes that live in lakes, streams, and marshes.

When autumn comes, the snakes of our northern states and Canada seek the warmer places in their areas. They often gather on southern hillsides and ledges. There they rest in the sun in order to warm their stiffened muscles before they set out to hunt for food.

As the weather grows colder, the snakes seek sheltered places to spend the winter.

GARTER, DE KAY's, and WATER SNAKES may choose deserted animal burrows or other holes in the ground.

BLACK SNAKES may go under boulders and MILK SNAKES into crevices between rocks. COPPERHEADS often winter in groups in rock crevices or hollows under roots or fallen trees. The SMOOTH GREEN SNAKE goes into stone walls and rotted stumps.

PILOT BLACK SNAKES live in hilly country and go into caves in winter. BULL SNAKES also winter in hillside caves.

RATTLERS congregate, often in large numbers, in the same dens every winter. The dens, in rocky caves or cavities in hills and river banks, may be shared with other kinds of snakes.

Before freezing weather comes, the snakes are all in their dens and ready to enter into a state of hibernation. Their bodies grow stiff and cold, their heartbeats and other functions slow down, and they become unconscious.

Sometimes groups of hibernating snakes are intertwined into a ball. This helps to conserve heat and moisture. There may be from two or three to hundreds of individual snakes, including more than one species, in a ball.

In spring as the weather grows warmer, the snakes awaken from their long sleep. They crawl out into the sun during the day but return to their dens at night. Finally, when warm weather comes to stay, they leave their dens and spread out over the countryside.

TURTLES

The turtle's body is covered wholly or in part by a large shell (carapace) on the back and a smaller one (plastron) on the underside. Most of its ribs are attached to the carapace. Both shells are bony and covered with horny plates. The turtle has large lungs that can store enough air to last for a long time. Those that live in the water do not have to come to the surface very often to take a gulp of air.

In autumn they become less active. Sometimes pond turtles swim slowly even under ice, but usually they hibernate when the water becomes cold. During hibernation the body functions of the turtle slow down. It does not have to breathe much, since it has air stored in its lungs. Also it is able to absorb oxygen from the water through some parts of its body.

The PAINTED TURTLE lives in weedy ponds across the United States and southern Canada. Its carapace is from six to eight inches long and is dark brown with yellow, red, and black markings. In early spring it swims or suns itself on logs or stones. In June it lays eggs in a hole that it digs in the ground near its pond. In summer the eggs usually hatch into inch-long turtles, but some late ones may not hatch until the following spring. In autumn painted turtles dig into the bottom mud of ponds and quiet streams, where they hibernate until spring.

The SPOTTED TURTLE is found in ponds in the eastern states. Its black carapace with yellow dots is about five inches long. In summer it lays from two to four eggs in a hole that it digs in the sandy shore. The eggs hatch into small turtles in September, when it is nearly time for those that live in the colder parts of their range to hibernate. The turtles dig into the mud at the bottom of a pond and remain there all winter.

The SNAPPING TURTLE, found in slow rivers, ponds, and lakes in eastern and central United States, is one of the largest. Its dull colored carapace, which does not cover all its body, grows to be a foot long. In summer the female turtle lays a dozen or more eggs in soft ground near the water. The eggs

PAINTED
TURTLE

SPOTTED
TURTLE

SNAPPING TURTLE

WOOD
TURTLE

BOX
TURTLE

Closed shell (underside)
of BOX TURTLE

either hatch in late summer or remain in their hole through the winter and hatch the following spring. In the colder parts of their range snapping turtles hibernate in mud underwater from late September or October until April.

The WOOD TURTLE is found in the northeastern parts of the United States and into Canada. Its carapace, which may be eight or nine inches long, is dull brown with some yellow markings. Ridges on each plate give it a rough sculptured appearance.

In spring the turtles go into water to mate, but they lay their eggs in the ground in sandy places. Eggs laid in June hatch at the end of summer.

During warm weather wood turtles live most of the time in fields, marshes, or woods, although they sometimes swim in brooks or ponds. In the fall they enter streams, and before cold weather comes, they dig into the muddy bottom. There they hibernate until around April.

The BOX TURTLE lives in the eastern and central states. Its high arched carapace grows about five inches long and is dark brown with yellow marks. Its plastron is hinged and can be closed tightly against the carapace to form a box with the turtle inside. Box turtles live on land in open brush-covered country, often staying in one area for a long time. In spring the females lay their eggs in shallow holes in the ground. The eggs hatch at the end of summer or in early fall, when it is nearly time for the turtles to hibernate.

In preparing for its winter sleep the box turtle eats more than usual of the plants, berries, and insects on which it feeds. As a result it may become so fat that it cannot completely close its shell. Before cold weather comes, the turtle finds a place where the soil is loose. At first it digs a few inches underground. Then, in the colder parts of its range, it continues to dig until it is below the frost line. There it withdraws into its shell and remains through the winter in such a dormant state that it appears to be dead. However, around April it returns to life and resumes its usual activities.

Birds

Many of the birds that live and nest in the northern part of our country and in Canada during the summer leave before cold weather comes in order to fly to a warmer climate where more food is available. A few members of some of these migrating species remain in the north when they can find food. Other species stay in the north throughout the year. In very severe weather all may have difficulty in getting enough to eat. Bird feeding stations that are kept stocked through the winter help to relieve the shortage.

Birds' feathers serve not only for flight but also as a protection in bad weather. The outer coat of contour feathers acts as a windbreaker and holds an insulating layer of air that serves to keep body heat.

In the fall some birds change their colors. The male goldfinch loses his bright yellow to become olive brown like the female. The black and white of the male bobolink changes to olive streaked with black, the coloring of the female. Many warblers that are brightly colored in summer become dull and hard to identify in the fall.

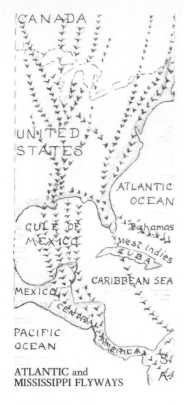

ATLANTIC and
MISSISSIPPI FLYWAYS

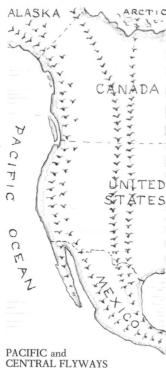

PACIFIC and
CENTRAL FLYWAYS

MIGRATION

Since birds are protected from the weather by their feathers, they do not suffer from the cold. Their winter problem is the lack of food. Birds that are able to remain in the north are those insect-eaters that can find hibernating insects and their larvae under bark, or seed- and berry-eaters that can exist on weed seeds and dry berries.

Birds that are not able to find enough to eat move to warmer climates where food is plentiful. Some travel only a short distance like mountain dwellers that go down to the valleys and others that make short easterly or westerly trips. Most of the migrants go farther — to the southern states, or to Central or South America. Each species goes to the same region every winter and returns to the same area every summer.

On the long journeys many birds lose their lives, some during storms or unseasonable weather. Some are attracted or confused by lights and fly against tall buildings, towers, or wires.

Some birds travel by day, but more of them travel at night. It is not known how they find their way. Some of the day fliers seem to adjust to the position of the sun. Some night fliers may navigate by noting the position of the stars. Some birds may have an instinctive sense of direction; others may remember landmarks. During a heavy fog or cloudiness many birds get lost.

Birds have been migrating for so long that it is now a hereditary instinct. Some start south before their food supply gives out and long before cold weather comes. They go as soon as the young that were raised during the summer are strong enough to make a long flight. Young birds, including some species of warblers, may travel without their parents. Cowbirds are raised in the nests of other birds and have no parents to guide them; yet they go to the wintering grounds of their ancestors.

In spring birds leave the south because they need more space to spread out when it is time to raise new families.

Birds travel southward by many routes. Favorite flyways follow the coasts, mountains, and rivers. Many flyways converge near the Gulf of Mexico. The birds fly across the Gulf to reach southern Mexico and Central America, usually traveling at night in order to feed before and after the flight. Other birds take off from Florida to go to the West Indies or on to South America. Some water birds travel all or most of the way to their wintering places by sea.

ARCTIC TERN

FARTHEST MIGRANTS

The ARCTIC TERN nests along the most northerly coasts of this hemisphere and spends the winter around the pack ice of the Antarctic. It makes the longest journey of any of the migrating birds, a trip of some eleven thousand miles. Traveling alone or in small groups, terns leave the islands of the far north and northern Canada, cross the Atlantic to the coast of Europe and Asia, then go along the coastline of South America and on to the Antarctic. From western Alaska terns go down the Pacific coast, and some may winter off the coast of Chile. The terns travel over the sea all the way to their destination. They feed by plunging into the water to catch fish, and they rest on the water or on floating debris. While they are in the north and in the south, the sun never sets, so terns have more hours of daylight in a year than any other bird.

The AMERICAN GOLDEN PLOVER, scarcely larger than a robin but with a wider wingspread, makes one of the longest journeys of any shorebird. It nests across the northern part of our continent and spends the winter from Brazil and Bolivia south to the pampas of Argentina. During its journey the plover flies over the Atlantic from Nova Scotia to northern South America, a nonstop flight of over two thousand miles. Plovers that nest in the Aleutians off the coast of Alaska make an equally long flight over the Pacific to Hawaii, then go on to more southern islands to spend the winter. In spring the plovers make the northward trip overland by way of Central America, Mexico, and the Mississippi Valley.

MIGRATION ROUTES

AMERICAN
GOLDEN PLOVER

EASTERN
BLUEBIRD

HOUSE WREN

HERMIT
THRUSH

RUFOUS

RUBY-
THROATED

HUMMINGBIRDS

RED-WINGED
BLACKBIRD

MIGRATORS TO SOUTHERN STATES AND MEXICO

1) The ROBIN of our east, west, and northwest winters along both coasts, in the southern states, and in Mexico.

2) The EASTERN BLUEBIRD winters in the southeastern quarter of the United States. 3) The WESTERN BLUEBIRD migrates toward lower California. 4) The MOUNTAIN BLUEBIRD winters in the southwestern states and northern Mexico.

5) The TREE SWALLOW winters along all our southern coasts, through Mexico into Central America, and in Cuba.

6) The CEDAR WAXWING winters across our country, except in the north central states, and in Mexico.

7) The GOLDEN-CROWNED KINGLET winters in most of the United States and into Mexico.

8) The RUBY-CROWNED KINGLET spends the winter in the southern states and Mexico.

9) The BROWN TOWHEE winters in the southwestern states. 10) The RUFOUS-SIDED TOWHEE winters across the southern states. Both also go into Mexico.

11) The WHITE-CROWNED SPARROW winters in most of the southern half of the United States and into Mexico. 12) The WHITE-THROATED SPARROW winters in the east and southeast. 13) The VESPER SPARROW winters in the southern states and Mexico, and so does 14) the CHIPPING SPARROW.

15) SAY'S PHOEBE winters in the southwestern states and Mexico. 16) The EASTERN PHOEBE winters in the southeastern and Gulf states and eastern Mexico.

17) RED-WINGED BLACKBIRDS winter in coastal and southern states and Mexico.

18) The BROWN THRASHER spends the winter in the southeastern and Gulf states.

19) The HERMIT THRUSH winters along the southwest coast, in the southern states, and in Mexico.

20) BROWN-HEADED COWBIRDS, old and young birds traveling separately, migrate to the southern states and Mexico.

21) HOUSE WRENS from our eastern and western states winter in Mexico.

22) The WESTERN KINGBIRD and 23) BULLOCK'S ORIOLE spend the winter in Mexico.

24) The WESTERN TANAGER spends the winter over most of Mexico and into Guatemala.

25) The RUBY-THROATED HUMMINGBIRD of the eastern states flies across the Gulf to Mexico and Central America.

26) The RUFOUS HUMMINGBIRD migrates through the western states on its way to Mexico.

ROBIN

BARN SWALLOW

OVENBIRD

BALTIMORE
ORIOLE

SCARLET
TANAGER

BOBOLINK

MIGRATORS TO CENTRAL AND SOUTH AMERICA

1) The BARN SWALLOW winters from California and the southern states through Mexico to Honduras and Cuba.

2) The CATBIRD winters in the southern states, through Mexico and Central America to the West Indies.

3) The WOOD THRUSH spends the winter in Central America and northern South America.

4) The OVENBIRD winters from the Gulf states, Mexico, and Central America to Colombia and the West Indies.

5) The BALTIMORE ORIOLE migrates to Mexico, Central America, and Colombia.

6) The ROSE-BREASTED GROSBEAK winters from southern Mexico to northwest South America.

7) The DICKCISSEL migrates through Mexico and Central America to Venezuela and Trinidad.

8) The RED-EYED VIREO winters in Ecuador, Venezuela, and southern Brazil.

9) The BLACK-AND-WHITE WARBLER winters from the Gulf states and Mexico south to northern South America.

10) CHIMNEY SWIFTS winter in west Brazil and east Peru.

11) The SCARLET TANAGER winters in the West Indies, Mexico, and Central America southward to Peru and Brazil.

12) The YELLOW WARBLER winters from southern Mexico to the Guianas, Brazil, and Peru.

13) The BLACKPOLL WARBLER migrates through the Bahamas and West Indies to Venezuela, the Guianas, and Brazil.

14) The AMERICAN REDSTART winters in the West Indies, Mexico, Central America, and northern South America.

15) The PURPLE MARTIN winters from southern Florida and Mexico southward to Brazil.

16) The EASTERN KINGBIRD winters in Costa Rica, Peru, and Bolivia.

17) BOBOLINKS winter in the meadows and marshes of Brazil, Bolivia, Paraguay, and northern Argentina.

18) The COMMON NIGHTHAWK migrates to Colombia, Brazil, and Argentina.

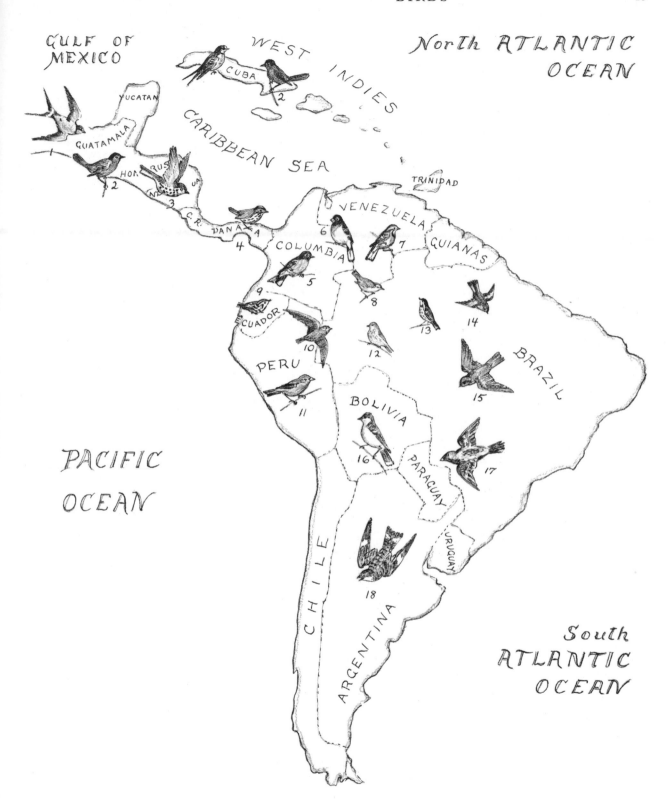

MYRTLE
WARBLER

AMERICAN
GOLDFINCH

PURPLE
FINCH

HORNED
LARK

MEADOW-
LARK

SOME STAY IN THE NORTH

Some members of migrating species, especially seed-eaters, remain in the north all winter if they can find food.

Some MYRTLE WARBLERS spend the winter in the eastern and western coastal states, while others go as far south as Mexico and Central America. On the northeastern coast they feed on the berries of myrtle (bayberry), red cedar, poison ivy, and others, as well as hibernating insects. The male in winter is brownish like the female with yellow on his rump.

The male AMERICAN GOLDFINCH loses his bright colors when cold weather comes and looks much like the olive-brown female. In the fall most goldfinches travel toward the southern states, but some remain in the north all winter if they can find seeds to eat. They often visit feeders for sunflower seeds.

PURPLE FINCHES are the same color winter and summer, the male a rosy red, the female a drab brown and white. In their eastern and western forms they live in Canada and the coastal states, moving southward and inland in winter. Those that stay in the north search for berries and weed seeds, or sunflower seeds in feeders.

The male HOUSE FINCH is more brownish on the back and reddish around the head than the purple finch. House finches are common year round in the west, and some now live in parts of southern New England. They eat seeds and fruit.

The HORNED LARK is streaked brown on the back, yellow around the face and throat with black markings, and has a black tail. It lives on prairies, fields, and shores from Canada to Mexico, leaving the most northerly part of its range in winter. It feeds on grain, weed seeds, and insects.

EASTERN and WESTERN MEADOWLARKS live in fields and other grassy places in the United States. Speckled brown on the back, they have white outer tail feathers and are yellow underneath with a black band on the throat. Some birds move southward in winter; some stay along both coasts where they are able to find some insects as well as weed seeds to eat.

Some insect-eating birds are able to remain in the north all winter by feeding on hibernating insects, insect eggs and pupae, and also suet and sunflower seeds in home feeders.

Chickadees are regular visitors to home feeders that contain sunflower seeds, suet, or peanut butter. Their natural food, insects, they pick out of the bark of trees, often hanging upside down in the process. BLACK-CAPPED CHICKADEES are found in Canada, the northern and central states, and southward in winter. The MOUNTAIN CHICKADEE of the west can be told from the black-capped by the white line over its eye.

Nuthatches search for insects in the bark of trees, often going down the trunk head first. In winter they also eat grain, sunflower seeds, and small nuts. Male and female remain together throughout the year and may be heard calling to each other. The WHITE-BREASTED NUTHATCH is found in southern Canada and the eastern half of the United States. The PYGMY NUTHATCH lives in the pine forests of western North America.

BROWN CREEPERS are little brown and white birds that spiral up tree trunks. They probe under bark with their thin, curved bills as they search for food. They nest in Canada, our northern states, and eastern and western mountains. In winter some remain in the north and some move southward.

Woodpeckers with their strong bills are able to gouge out insects that the smaller birds are unable to reach. They also use their bills to dig out a nesting or sleeping hole in the trunk of a tree. DOWNY and HAIRY WOODPECKERS are black and white birds, the hairy being the larger of the two. They live in Canada and most of the United States.

Flickers are large, brownish woodpeckers. The YELLOW-SHAFTED FLICKER of Canada and the eastern states has yellow under its wings and tail. In winter it leaves the most northerly part of its range. The RED-SHAFTED FLICKER has red under its wings and tail. It lives all year in the western states.

BLUE JAYS are well known throughout the year in all but the western states. In winter they eat acorns and nuts and visit feeders, which they quickly empty of seeds and peanuts.

BLACK-CAPPED CHICKADEE

WHITE-BREASTED NUTHATCH

BROWN CREEPER

DOWNY WOODPECKER

FLICKER

BLUE JAY

VARIED
THRUSH

STELLER'S
JAY

GRAY JAY

CLARK'S
NUT-
CRACKER

BLACK-BILLED MAGPIE

THESE LIVE IN THE NORTHWEST

The VARIED THRUSH is a robin-like bird with a black band on its breast. It nests in the spruce forests of mountains along the northern Pacific coast. When snowstorms drive it into the valleys, it may be found as far south as southern California. In fall and winter it eats fruits and will stay where they are available.

STELLER'S JAYS are dark blue on the lower back and tail, black on the head and shoulders, and they have a long crest. They live all the year in evergreen forests of the northern Pacific coastal area. Related species live in more southerly western and central states. In fall and winter the jays eat seeds, acorns, and berries. In spring and summer they also eat some animal food, including bird eggs.

The CALIFORNIA SCRUB JAY is blue with a brownish back and a white throat. It does not have a crest. It nests in scrub oak or piñon pine. Related species live in other Pacific and western states. Like other jays, their diet includes fruit and some animal food.

The GRAY JAY, another crestless bird, is gray except for a white head with a dark patch on top or back. Subspecies live in Alaska, Canada, and the Rocky Mountains. They nest in evergreen forests. They eat insects, small animal life, and garbage or food found near homes and camps.

CLARK'S NUTCRACKER looks like a small crow with a gray body, black and white wings and tail. It nests in evergreen forests in high mountains of western North America. In winter flocks may wander southward or down to the coast. Besides insects, it feeds on acorns, nuts, seeds from pine cones, the berries of cedar and juniper, and camp scraps. Around camps it may become tame enough to feed from the hand.

BLACK-BILLED MAGPIES are large black and white birds with long tails. They live throughout the year in sparsely wooded areas of western North America, sometimes in large colonies. Noisy birds, they chatter continuously. They feed on insects, fruit, green leaves, and small animal life.

IRREGULAR WINTER VISITORS

These birds nest in far northern forests. In winter they wander into our northern states and sometimes farther south. They usually travel in flocks and stop where they can find weed or tree seeds to eat. Many of them may be seen in a place one winter and not again for several years.

COMMON REDPOLLS look like light sparrows with a red patch on the forehead, and the males have pink on the breast. Flocks are seen in winter woods, fields, or around feeders.

PINE SISKINS are like small brown striped sparrows with yellow on wings and tail that shows only in flight. In winter they collect in large flocks and roam in search of cones, tree and weed seeds, and also visit bird feeders.

The crossbill uses its curious bill to get at the seeds of pine and other cones. By inserting its closed bill into the cone and then opening it, the bird forces the cone to spread out. Strong jaw muscles help in the process. After the seeds are exposed, the bird scoops them out with its tongue. It can also cut up an apple in order to get the seeds.

The RED CROSSBILL male is dull red with brownish wings and tail; the female is a mottled yellowish brown. Flocks of a few dozen to several hundred wander from forest to forest and sometimes visit towns with coniferous or fruit trees.

The WHITE-WINGED CROSSBILL male has a rosy red body, black wings and tail, and white wing bars. The female is brownish and yellow and has two white wing bars.

The PINE GROSBEAK is a heavy billed bird that is gray with a pinkish back in the male and yellowish brown in the female. Flocks visit our northern and middle states once in a while when cones become scarce in Canadian forests.

The EVENING GROSBEAK, a stocky bird, is striking in color, at least the male, which is yellow, brown, black, and white. Flocks of these birds travel from west to east as well as from far north southward in winter. They are especially fond of dry fruits found on vines, shrubs, and trees and may visit house yards that have juniper, fruit trees, hedges, or sunflower seeds.

COMMON REDPOLL

PINE SISKIN

RED and WHITE-WINGED CROSSBILLS

PINE and EVENING GROSBEAKS

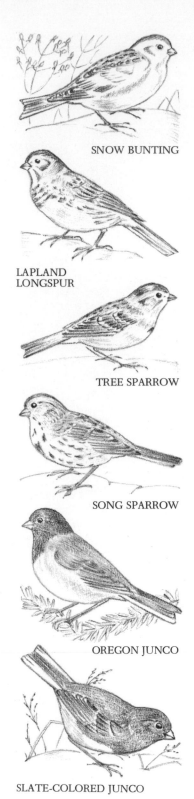

SNOW BUNTING

LAPLAND
LONGSPUR

TREE SPARROW

SONG SPARROW

OREGON JUNCO

SLATE-COLORED JUNCO

NORTHERN SPARROWS

Most of these sparrows nest in Canada or the far north. In winter they are seen in our northern states, where they feed on the seeds of weeds and grasses or visit feeders. The two that come from the farthest north and are irregular winter visitors are the snow bunting and the Lapland longspur.

SNOW BUNTINGS in summer are white with black markings. In winter they have a brownish tinge on the back. They are seen on snowy hillsides in the east and on western prairies. Large flocks fly together, and the birds whistle to each other.

The LAPLAND LONGSPUR, light brown streaked with black on the back, is black on the head and chest in summer, lighter in winter. In midwinter flocks live on prairies and meadows of the central states and some along the east coast.

The TREE SPARROW, brownish above and light underneath, has a reddish-brown crown and a small dark spot on the breast. Flocks of these birds are seen in the western as well as northern states in winter. They are as much "ground" as "tree" sparrows.

SONG SPARROWS can be identified by their streaked sides and large dark spot on the breast. They nest in southern Canada and all the United States. Some of them remain in the northern states throughout the year. On mild days in winter they start to sing their spring song.

The FOX SPARROW is larger and more heavily streaked than the song sparrow, and the eastern kind is more reddish brown. A few eastern sparrows stay in the north; most go to the middle or southern states. The western fox sparrow winters in the Pacific states.

The OREGON JUNCO has a black head, reddish-brown back, and buffy sides. It nests in the forests of western Canada and the United States and winters in the Pacific states.

SLATE-COLORED JUNCOS are dark gray above and white underneath. In the fall they move southward in flocks. Some spend the winter in the northern states; others go as far as Florida and New Mexico.

NORTHERN GAME BIRDS

The BOBWHITE, a small quail found in most of the eastern half of the United States, remains throughout the year in the same area. It is a short-tailed, stout little bird that runs like a chicken. A family group is sometimes seen in summer. The family stays together through the winter and usually joins others to make a covey. At night the covey forms a circle on the ground. The birds sleep with their tails pointing in and their heads pointing outward. If disturbed, they all fly out in different directions. While they are sleeping, their bodies are pressed together to conserve heat. If a heavy snow falls and an icy crust forms during the night, the birds may be imprisoned and die. Heavy snow may also cover the food supply and cause starvation. Quail eat weed seeds and dry fruits. They like corn put out for them and also grit or coarse sand.

BOB-WHITE

The RUFFED GROUSE has a crest on the head, a ruff on the neck, and varied markings in shades of brown, gray, and buff. It lives in southern Canada and our northern and eastern states, staying in the same area throughout the year. Larger and stronger than the quail, it is better able to withstand the cold. Also it makes special preparations for winter by putting on a layer of fat, and a comblike growth on the sides of its toes that enables it to walk over the snow.

It can dig into the snow to find seeds, but it usually feeds in trees, where it eats buds, berries, dried fruits, and the needles of evergreens. At night the grouse dives into the snow and sleeps alone under it. In the morning it breaks out and returns to its perch in a tree.

RUFFED GROUSE

The male RING-NECKED PHEASANT with his glossy greenish head, white neck band, variegated reddish and brown body colors, and long tail is one of our most beautiful birds. The female is brownish. Natives of Asia, pheasants have become naturalized in some of our northern states, where they are able to live throughout the year if the winters are not too severe. They like open woodlands or fields where they can feed on weed seeds, grain, and berries.

RING-NECKED
PHEASANT

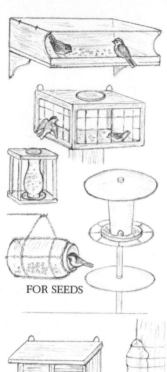

FOR SEEDS

FOR SEEDS OR SUET

GROUND FEEDER

FEEDING STATIONS

If you set up a feeding station near your home, you will be able to watch the winter birds from a window. You will be surprised to see how many different kinds will come as soon as they become accustomed to a new eating place. During fall and spring you will see migrating birds; in winter, those that stay in the north. Once you have started a feeder, it is important to continue it throughout the cold weather, since some birds may become dependent upon it.

There are many kinds of feeders that you can buy or make. Wooden platform or box type feeders attach to windowsills, poles, or trees. Hanging feeders may be made from large glass jars, small hollow logs, a log with holes bored in it, cut down milk containers, net vegetable bags, and pine cones. A shelter on the ground may be made from evergreen branches.

If you have different kinds of feeders, you will attract many kinds of birds. The feeders should be located on the sunny side of the house, preferably near shrubs or trees.

To fill the feeders, use wild birdseed or sunflower seed from a produce store, or food from the kitchen, such as rolled oats, bread or cornbread crumbs, and stale doughnuts; dried squash, pumpkin, and melon seeds, and apple cores with seeds; popcorn, peanuts, and cracked nuts; grapes, raisins, and cranberries. Pieces of suet may be put in net bags and hung from branches. Pine cones hung from a string may be spread with peanut butter mixed with fat or cornmeal. Taken alone, peanut butter may cause choking.

For scattering on the ground you can get baby chick scratch feed and cracked corn from a poultry supply store. When the ground is covered with snow and ice, the birds need some form of grit to help digest their food. Coarse sand or ashes will serve the purpose. For drinking and bathing, birds need water, which may be put in a shallow bowl near their food. In winter they drink some melted ice and snow.

If you grow trees and shrubs that have berries which last through the winter, birds will come to eat the berries.

Mammals

Mammals are animals that nourish their young on mother's milk. All that live in North America bear their young alive. Mammals have hair, and many have fur coats that are heavy enough to give protection from cold and moisture. Since they are warm-blooded creatures, mammals can maintain their body temperature regardless of changes in the weather.

As with birds, their biggest problem in winter is to find enough to eat. Mammals that feed on green plants and some that eat grain or insects are not able to find sufficient food. They solve the problem by eating heavily in summer in order to put on an extra layer of fat. This serves as nourishment while they sleep through the cold weather. By the time spring comes they may be very lean.

Only a few mammals in our area, such as some species of bats, migrate to warmer places.

Meat-eating mammals that prey on smaller creatures continue to hunt throughout the winter. Those that eat bark, twigs, and roots usually remain active also. But all may have to travel farther than usual to find food.

Hibernating

LITTLE BROWN BATS

CHIPMUNK   Hibernating

Hibernating

JUMPING MOUSE

HIBERNATORS

True hibernators pass the winter in such a deep sleep that they almost seem to be dead. Their heartbeat and their breathing are very slow. Their temperature is far below normal, so they must sleep in a sheltered place, often an underground den that is deeper than the frost line.

Early in fall LITTLE BROWN BATS seek places to spend the winter. Large numbers gather in caves, smaller groups in hollow trees or in buildings. They sleep head down, hanging by their feet with their wings folded against their bodies. Their temperature drops, and their breathing slows down. They are rather easily awakened, however, being disturbed by touch, vibration, or change in temperature. From time to time, in a cave a few bats awaken and fly around.

BIG BROWN BATS usually seek shelter in buildings.

The home of the EASTERN CHIPMUNK is an underground tunnel with several rooms, the largest being the bedroom. Before cold weather comes, the chipmunk puts a supply of seeds and nuts in its bedroom and makes a bed of grass or leaves on top of them. About the time of the first frost it retires. In warm spells during the winter it feeds from its food supply, but in the coldest weather it sleeps soundly with its body curled up and its tail around its head and back. It becomes cold and stiff and has a slow pulse. When early spring comes, it warms up, awakens, and sets out to find a mate.

WESTERN CHIPMUNKS that live where winters are cold have the same general hibernating habits as the eastern kind, but they may not remain inside as long.

JUMPING MICE live in Canada and the northern part of our country. Since they are nocturnal, they are not often seen, although they may be common in fields and woods in some areas. Their summer home is a nest of leaves or grass on or under the ground or in a shrub. Early in the fall each mouse retires to an underground den where it curls up and sleeps with its tail wound around its body. Early in spring it awakens and emerges regardless of weather to search for a mate.

Many kinds of GROUND SQUIRRELS live in the western part of North America. They are striped, spotted, or a solid color, and they have long, short, flattened, or rounded tails. They vary in size from that of a chipmunk to a tree squirrel. Living in valleys, mountains, fields, woods, and deserts, they make homes in underground burrows. Their food consists of seeds, nuts, and fruits, some of which they store for future use. Many that live in cold areas put on extra fat to serve as nourishment during hibernation. Some kinds remain underground most of the year.

The COLUMBIAN GROUND SQUIRREL retires during the dry season in summer, when green plants become scarce. Although it has a store of seeds and bulbs, it usually does not eat until it awakens toward the end of February, the mating time.

STRIPED GROUND SQUIRRELS retire in late summer or fall, the fattest ones first. Although they awaken at intervals during the winter, only a few in warmer places go outside.

GOLDEN-MANTLED GROUND SQUIRRELS in cold areas may stay in their dens from September until April. Restless hibernators, they may wake up for a day or two now and then.

The MARMOTS and WOODCHUCK are large relatives of the ground squirrels. Marmots live in rocky, hilly, or mountainous areas in western North America. Their home is a den under a rock or tree, or in a rocky cliff near a meadow. The woodchuck lives in open woods or fields across the central part of the United States and Canada. Its underground home usually consists of several tunnels and dens.

Marmots and woodchucks eat plants and some insects. In late summer they stuff themselves to put on extra fat, which will nourish them in their long winter sleep. When the weather begins to grow cold, they retire to their underground burrows and curl up. True hibernators, they remain in a deep sleep, unaware of touch or sound. Those that live in the colder parts sleep for six months or longer. In late winter or early spring they slowly awaken. Soon after emerging above ground, each one sets out to find a mate.

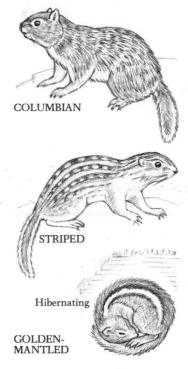

COLUMBIAN

STRIPED

Hibernating

GOLDEN-
MANTLED

GROUND SQUIRRELS

WOODCHUCK

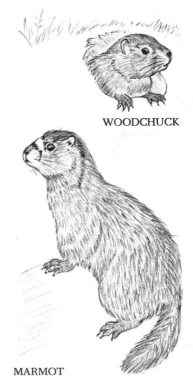

MARMOT

PRAIRIE DOG

BADGER

Sleeping

BLACK BEAR

HIBERNATORS AND SLEEPERS

PRAIRIE DOGS are ground squirrels that live in the west, the BLACK-TAILED kind in open, flat, dry areas of the High Plains, the WHITE-TAILED kind usually in higher altitudes of the Rocky Mountains. Their homes are in colonies or villages composed of tunnels with underground chambers. On sunny days the animals emerge to feed on nearby vegetation and insects. In bad weather they stay inside. In winter the black-tailed kind usually remains active. The white-tailed kind hibernates. After eating to become fat, it retires to its grass-lined bedroom far underground, where it remains until the mating season in late winter or early spring.

BADGERS live in dry areas with ground squirrels and prairie dogs, on which they prey. In the northern part of its range the badger eats to put on extra fat before cold weather, but this is not enough to sustain it all winter. When it is hungry, it goes out hunting regardless of weather. A strong digger, the badger claws its prey out of their burrows. It quickly and easily digs a burrow for itself and has a winter home in a den at the end of a long tunnel.

BLACK BEARS live in wooded areas throughout North America. They feed on fruits, nuts, and other vegetation, also on small animals. In the fall they eat heavily to put on a layer of fat. When cold weather comes, they seek sheltered places under logs or in a cave, although a male bear may lie in the snow protected by his heavy coat of glossy fur. Although bears sleep through most of the cold weather, they are not true hibernators, since their temperature and breathing remain normal. Female bears that are about to become mothers make a nest of dry leaves in a secure den. Here, toward the end of winter while still half asleep, they deliver their one or two, occasionally three, cubs. The cubs feed on their mother's milk, but the mother does not eat until spring, when the family leaves the den. They live in the open until the following winter; then the mother and partly grown cubs either sleep together or in nearby dens.

PART-TIME SLEEPERS

These animals sleep in a sheltered place through the coldest winter weather, but they are not true hibernators. Their temperature, heartbeat, and breathing do not fall below normal. Usually they are easily awakened. Sometimes they leave their dens to go out looking for food in mild weather, although most of them have put on an extra layer of fat to serve as winter nourishment.

RACCOONS live in wooded places near water in most of North America. They feed at night on fruit, grain, insects, small water animals, and sometimes garbage found near houses. Those that live in the north sleep in hollow trees or other shelter, often one or more families together. At the end of winter the mating season brings them out even when snow is on the ground. The flat-footed prints that they leave in the snow resemble the handprints and footprints of a small child.

RACCOONS

STRIPED SKUNK

OPOSSUM

The STRIPED SKUNK is common in the eastern states. Related species live in other parts of our country and Canada. In the north skunks sleep in a den such as a former woodchuck hole, a tunnel that they dig, or under a building. Dry leaves and grass are used to make a bed and to plug the doorway. Some skunks stay alone, some in a family or other group. By February or March the adults are out and ready to mate. Their footprints in the snow show the soles of the feet with claw marks on the front, but usually not on the hind feet.

OPOSSUMS live in wooded areas in the eastern and southern states. They are more numerous in the south but are extending their range in the northern states. In the south they are active throughout the year, feeding at night in trees or on the ground. They feed on fruit, vegetables, insects, other small animals, and anything else that is edible. In winter in the north they sleep in hollow trees, woodpiles, or other shelter, including cellars of houses. Once in a while they venture out, even in snowy weather. Their prints on the snow show the spread toes of the forefeet, the grasping inner toe of the hind feet, and a long tail mark between footprints.

FLYING SQUIRREL

RED SQUIRREL

GRAY SQUIRREL

FOX SQUIRREL

ACTIVE ON THE GROUND AND IN TREES

Squirrels are out in good weather all winter looking for food or using supplies that they have stored in the fall. On stormy or unusually cold days they stay in their nests in hollow trees or other shelter. As they bound over the snow, they leave paired tracks that show the larger hind feet in front of the small forefeet. The end of winter is mating season, and the first family is born in early spring.

FLYING SQUIRRELS live in woods over much of North America, but since they are active only at night, they are not often seen. The northern variety is larger than the eastern, but both are small and weigh only a few ounces. Their silky fur is brownish or grayish on the back and light underneath. A fold of fur-covered skin stretched between the fore and hind legs enables the squirrel to glide with legs outspread from tree to tree. The flattened furry tail helps to steer up or down. In winter the squirrels eat tender bark, hibernating insects, and nuts or seeds from trees or stored supplies.

The CHICKAREE, OR RED SQUIRREL, is more brownish or grayish in winter, and its ears have tufts of dusky hairs. It eats pine cones, dry fruit, tree buds, seeds, nuts, and mushrooms. Some mushrooms are stored in tree branches to dry. Seeds and nuts are stored in holes in trees or in the ground.

The EASTERN GRAY SQUIRREL is seen in parks and gardens as well as in the woods. In winter it has white tufts on the back of its ears. It eats acorns, hickory and other nuts, some of which it stores in the ground for future use. Its sense of smell helps it to find them again. Even when the ground is covered with snow, it is able to locate them.

The WESTERN GRAY SQUIRREL, similar in appearance and habits to the eastern but less numerous, lives in oak and pine forests on mountain slopes of the Pacific coast.

The FOX SQUIRREL, larger and heavier than the gray, varies in color from buff or orange to gray or dark brown. It has similar habits and lives in the same area as the eastern gray, but it is seldom as numerous.

Although the PORCUPINE is a slow and rather clumsy animal, it can climb a tree easily. In winter it may stay in one for days. Sitting on a branch, it gnaws at the bark, discarding the outer part and eating the soft inner layer. It also eats the needles from pine, spruce, and hemlock trees. Protected by its heavy coat of fine underfur overlaid by long, coarse guard hairs, it can withstand sub-zero weather. A den under rocks or a hollow tree or log serves as a shelter which several porcupines may share. When it travels over the snow, the bow-legged animal leaves flat-footed prints that toe inward.

Porcupines live in woods throughout North America. The eastern kind is dark brownish, the western yellowish.

PORCUPINE

ACTIVE ON THE GROUND

The COMMON MOLE of the eastern and central states lives in an underground tunnel throughout the year. In summer the tunnel is near the surface; in winter it is deeper. Using its wide front feet as shovels, the mole can dig more than a hundred feet during a night. In the tunnel it hunts day or night for insects, grubs, and worms to eat.

SHREWS live under fallen leaves or underbrush in the summer, in tunnels in the snow or in mouse or mole underground runways in winter. Nervous, active little creatures, they eat voraciously. Insects, worms, snails, mice sometimes larger than themselves, as well as some grain and nuts are part of their diet. Their digestion is rapid, and they may eat two or three times their own weight in a day.

The PIGMY SHREW, found across Canada and the northern part of the United States, is the smallest mammal in its area. Three or four inches long, half of which length is tail, it weighs only 1/14 ounce. The COMMON SHREW, only slightly larger than the pigmy, lives in woods and fields over most of North America. The SHORT-TAILED SHREW is four or five inches long and stockier than the other two. It lives in the eastern half of North America and is the only mammal on the continent whose bite is poisonous.

COMMON MOLE

SHORT-
TAILED
SHREW

MEADOW MOUSE

GRASSHOPPER
MOUSE

HARVEST MOUSE

WHITE-FOOTED
MOUSE

ACTIVE MICE

The MEADOW MOUSE is chunky, short-tailed, and from five to seven inches long including the tail. It has small eyes and ears. Different species live throughout the continent. The eastern kind is brown sprinkled with black in summer, gray in winter. In summer it makes runways through grass or weeds and underground tunnels. In winter it makes tunnels through the snow and runs through them to find seeds, stems, and roots to eat. It also eats the inner bark of trees. In winter it has a nest of dry grass underground or in snow.

The GRASSHOPPER MOUSE is another stocky, short-tailed mouse. From 5½ to 6½ inches long, it is grayish, brownish, or buff on the back and white underneath. It lives in grassy or sandy plains and foothills of western North America. Its nest is in an underground burrow. In winter, although it has become very plump and has stored some supplies, it is out at night searching for seeds, berries, and hibernating insects. In summer it also eats small mammals and many grasshoppers.

The HARVEST MOUSE looks like a small house mouse except that it is browner and has a more hairy tail. It lives in grassy, weedy places across the central part of our country and southward. It stores seeds but is active all winter searching through the snow for more seeds, weeds, or berries. Some harvest mice live underground, some in holes in trees, but most make their rounded, grassy nests in a dense growth of weeds or in low bushes.

The WHITE-FOOTED MOUSE and its relatives are found in most of North America. It is brownish or grayish on the back and white underneath. About four inches in body length, it has a tail that is almost as long. Its winter home is a nest of grass or other soft material in a hole in a tree, log, or sometimes in a building. Near its nest the mouse has a store of seeds, acorns, berries, shelled beechnuts, or other food. Active all winter, it runs about at night through tunnels in the snow or over the surface. It leaves dainty paired footprints with a long tail mark showing between them.

ACTIVE IN PONDS

The MUSKRAT is an oversized rat that lives in weedy ponds, streams, and marshes. With partly webbed feet to use as paddles and a long scaly, vertically flattened tail to act as a rudder, the muskrat is an expert swimmer. Its dense underfur covered by long, dark brown guard hairs protects it from cold and moisture. In the winter it swims under ice to find water weeds and roots, crayfish, fish, freshwater clams, and mussels to eat. If the water freezes solid, the muskrat travels over ground or snow and eats dry grasses, weeds, and willow twigs. Its footprints show the hind foot slightly in front of the fore-foot and a long tail line between them.

In a high-banked stream the muskrat makes its home in a burrow in the bank. In a marsh it makes a lodge by piling up grasses, cattails, and other plants and plastering them with mud. Then it digs a tunnel underneath and hollows out a sleeping room above water. Each muskrat has its own home except when mother and young are together and in cold weather when several adults may huddle together for warmth. Sometimes muskrats live in the walls of a beaver lodge.

The BEAVER weighs fifty or more pounds and is the largest rodent in North America. It lives in a pond that it makes by building a dam across a stream. The dam is made of logs, roots, and debris filled in with mud. In the fall the beaver strengthens the dam. It also fells small trees that it cuts up and stores underwater for a winter food supply.

The beaver's home sometimes is a burrow in the bank of a stream, but more often is a lodge made of sticks and mud in shallow water. The living quarters are above water, and the entrance tunnels are under water. Several beavers, sometimes the parents and last two sets of young, may live in one lodge. When the pond freezes over, the beaver swims under the ice to the stored logs, brings one back to the lodge, and gnaws on the bark in comfort. Its outer coat of oily hairs over dense underfur protects it from the cold water. Its large webbed hind feet and its broad, flat tail help in swimming.

MUSKRAT

BEAVER

RABBITS ARE ACTIVE

COTTONTAIL RABBIT

SNOWSHOE RABBIT

JACK RABBIT

COTTONTAIL RABBITS are found throughout the United States. Active at dawn and dusk except in stormy weather, the cottontail is often seen in gardens as well as at the edge of woods. Its summer home is a hollow, or form, under grass or shrubs. In winter it takes shelter under brush, in a rocky den, or in an underground burrow. Its winter food consists of dry weeds, buds and needles of evergreens, and the bark of many kinds of trees. Late in winter during the mating season the cottontails are especially active. As they bound over the ground, they balance on their front feet and bring their hind feet forward as their footprints show.

The SNOWSHOE RABBIT, or VARYING HARE, lives in woods in the colder parts of North America. Like other hares, it has long ears and long hind legs. In the fall it sheds its brown coat and starts to grow a white one, taking about ten weeks in the process. Its feet, ears, and front of head usually turn white before its back does. In further preparation for winter it grows long hairs between the spreading toes on its large hind feet, which then serve as snowshoes to keep the hare from sinking into deep snow. Its tracks can be told from those of the cottontail by their larger size.

In winter the hare feeds on buds, twigs, and the bark of shrubs and trees, especially willows, reaching as high as it can by standing on tiptoe. Its home is a form in a raised place on the ground sheltered by overhanging branches.

JACK RABBITS are hares that live in the western part of the United States and Canada. They are larger than the varying hare and grayer in color. The kinds that live on the plains have black on the upper part of their tail, and they do not change color in winter. The kinds that have white tails have lighter coats in winter, and those that live in the north or at high altitudes turn white. In the north their home may be a burrow in the snow. Farther south it is likely to be a form under grass, weeds, or bushes, or in the open. Jack rabbits are hearty eaters and may devour crops and winter hay.

DEER ARE ACTIVE

When cold weather comes, deer gather into herds. The bucks are peaceful now that the fall mating season is past. At the end of winter they lose their antlers and in spring start to grow new ones. Before winter comes, the deer's thin brown summer coat is replaced by a heavier, more grayish one.

In winter deer eat the bark and twigs of trees and the foliage of evergreens as far up as they can reach. They may also paw through snow to find grass, acorns, weeds, moss, or other vegetable food on the ground. A very heavy snow cover removes this source of food and also makes it difficult for the deer to move around.

WHITE-TAILED DEER live in most of North America with the exception of the desert states and the Pacific coast. Their tails, grayish on top and white underneath, are raised like white banners when the animals run. These deer spend the winter in a sheltered place in the woods or sometimes in a cedar swamp. They tramp down the snow to form a yard and also make long trails through the snow. They browse on the trees that border the yard and trails. At night the deer sleep in depressions that they make in the snow, choosing a different spot each time, since the previous one is apt to ice over.

BLACK-TAILED DEER live along the Pacific coast. They have brushlike tails that are black on the upper surface and light underneath. The deer that spend the summer in mountain areas move to valleys in winter. Those that live on northern islands move to the coast in winter, where they often become easy prey for their enemies.

MULE DEER are larger than the other two. They have big ears and large, doubly branched antlers. The tail, set in a white rump patch, is rounded and white with a black tip. These deer are found in western United States and southwest Canada. In summer they live in mountains among aspen, pine, or other open forests. When snowy weather comes, the herds drift down to valleys or foothills. There may be thirty miles or more between their summer and winter ranges.

WHITE-TAILED DEER

BLACK-TAILED DEER

MULE DEER

HEADS AND TAILS

WEASEL

MINK

OTTER

ACTIVE HUNTERS

WEASELS are agile little animals that live in woods, fields, and around farms. Fierce fighters, they not only feed on small creatures like insects and mice, but also attack and kill animals larger than themselves. Usually they do not travel far from home, which is a den under ground, roots, or rocks, often taken from a victim and lined with its fur or feathers.

The several kinds of weasels vary in size from six to twenty inches in total length. In warm weather they are brown on the back and white underneath. In the fall they molt, and those that live in cold climates replace their brown fur with white except the tip of the tail, which remains dark in all species but the least weasel, which is all white. White weasel fur with the black-tipped tail is sold under the name of ermine.

The MINK is a large weasel. Its fur is the same color winter and summer, dark brown except for a white patch under the chin. In winter it is sometimes seen along the bank of a partly frozen stream, darting in and out of the water. It can swim, bound rapidly over land, or climb trees. Hunting both day and night, it preys on many kinds of animals, some larger than itself.

The mink's den is in the bank of a stream, but usually it does not have a permanent home except when raising a family. Mink are trapped for their soft fur. Many also are raised on farms for the fur industry.

The OTTER is a large, long-bodied animal that lives near fresh water, where it feeds on fish and other water creatures. In winter it can swim under ice, travel over the surface, or tunnel through banks of snow. Protected by dense underfur and coarse outer fur and by a layer of fat on its body, it does not mind cold or moisture. Its home, in the bank of a stream, is a burrow with a bedroom at the top and an entrance under water. February is mating time, and the young are born in the spring. The young otters stay with the mother most of the year. A favorite sport of the whole family is sliding down a mud or snow bank into the water.

The MARTEN, a large relative of the weasel, can travel swiftly through the trees or over the ground. A tireless hunter, it preys on squirrels, birds, rabbits, mice, and other small creatures. It lives in evergreen forests in Canada, our northeastern states and western mountains. Although usually a shy animal, it is sometimes seen around campsites searching for garbage. Its soft durable fur is valuable.

MARTEN

The LYNX looks like a large cat with tufted ears, long ruff, and short tail. Its heavy fur is gray and brownish with black markings. In the northern evergreen forests where it lives it hunts at night throughout the year. Its prey consists of small animals, especially the snowshoe rabbit. Like the rabbit, the lynx has natural snowshoes as the result of a thick growth of hair on the sides and soles of its large feet. Besides being able to walk over the snow, it can climb trees and can swim if necessary. Ordinarily a quiet animal, it caterwauls loudly at mating time in late winter.

The BOBCAT is smaller than the lynx, and its feet do not keep it from sinking into deep snow. It lives throughout the United States and across both borders in all kinds of habitats. It preys on other animals, some larger than itself.

LYNX

The RED FOX lives in Canada and the United States except the southern states and the west coast. It hunts at dusk through woods and fields for small animals and sometimes dried fruits to eat. Through the first part of winter it lives alone and does not have a special home, sleeping under logs, rocks, or in the snow. Its heavy fur coat and bushy tail, which lies over its nose when it curls up, protect it from the cold. At the end of winter it seeks a mate and a den among rocks or tree roots. The young are born in the spring, and the family stays together until the following winter.

GRAY FOXES are more numerous in the south, but they are extending their range in the northern states. The fox family breaks up at the end of summer, but pairs stay together all year. They remain active and hunt throughout the winter. They are more shy and nocturnal than the red fox.

RED FOX

AMPHIBIANS AND REPTILES

Bishop, Sherman C. *Handbook of Salamanders*. New York: Hafner Publishing Company, 1962

Carr, Archie. *Handbook of Turtles: The Turtles of the United States, Canada, and Baja California*. Ithaca: Cornell University Press (Comstock Pubs.), 1952

Conant, Roger. *A Field Guide to Reptiles and Amphibians*. Boston: Houghton-Mifflin Company, 1958

Ditmars, Raymond L. *A Field Book of North American Snakes*. New York: Doubleday & Company, 1939

Stebbins, Robert C. *Amphibians and Reptiles of Western North America*. New York: McGraw-Hill Book Company, 1954

Wright, Albert H., and Wright, Anna A. *Handbook of Frogs and Toads of the United States and Canada*. Ithaca: Cornell University Press (Comstock Pubs.), 1949

BIRDS

Dorst, Jean. *The Migration of Birds*. Boston: Houghton, Mifflin & Company, 1962

Griffin, Donald R. *Bird Migration*. New York: Doubleday & Company, 1964

McElroy, Jr., Thomas P. *The New Handbook of Attracting Birds*. New York: Alfred A. Knopf, Inc., 1960

Peterson, Roger Tory. *A Field Guide to the Birds*. Boston: Houghton-Mifflin Company, 1947

Peterson, Roger Tory. *A Field Guide to Western Birds*. Boston: Houghton-Mifflin Company, 1961

Pettingill, Jr., Olin. *A Guide to Bird Finding East of the Mississippi*. New York: Oxford University Press, 1951

Pough, Richard H. *Audubon Land Bird Guide (eastern)*. New York: Doubleday & Company, 1949

Pough, Richard H. *Audubon Western Bird Guide*. New York: Doubleday & Company, 1957

Pough, Richard H. *Audubon Water Bird Guide: Water, Game, and Large Land Birds*. New York: Doubleday & Company, 1951

Robbins, Chandler; Bruun, B.; and Zim, H. S. *Birds of North America: A Guide to Field Identification*. New York: Golden Press, 1966

FISHES

Breder, Charles M. *Marine Fishes of the Atlantic Coast*. New York: G. P. Putnam's Sons, 1948

Eddy, Samuel, and Surber, Thaddeus. *Northern Fishes*. Boston: Charles T. Branford Company, 1947

Fichter, George S. *Fishes*. New York: Golden Press, 1963

LaMonte, Francesca. *North American Game Fishes*. New York: Doubleday & Company, 1958

Ommannev, F. D. and others. *The Fishes*. Morristown: Silver Burdett Company (Life Nature Library), 1963

Perlmutter, Alfred. *Guide to Marine Fishes*. New York: New York University Press, 1961

Shultz, Leonard P., and others. *Wondrous World of Fishes*. Washington, D.C.: National Geographic Society, 1965

Zim, Herbert S., and Shoemaker, Hurst H. *Fishes*. New York: Golden Press, 1957

INSECTS

Hussey, Lois J., and Pessino, Catherine. *Collecting Cocoons*. New York: Thomas Y. Crowell Company, 1953

Hutchins, Ross E. *Insects*. New York: Prentice-Hall Company, 1966

Klots, Alexander B. *A Field Guide to the Butterflies*. Boston: Houghton-Mifflin Company, 1951

Lutz, Frank E. *Field Book of Insects*. New York: G. P. Putnam's Sons, 1948

Mitchell, Robert, and Zim, Herbert S. *Butterflies and Moths*. New York: Golden Press, 1963

Swain, Ralph B. *The Insect Guide*. New York: Doubleday & Company, 1948

Teale, Edwin Way. *Junior Book of Insects*. New York: E. P. Dutton Company, 1953

Zim, Herbert S., and Cotton, Clarence. *Insects*. New York: Golden Press, 1951

MAMMALS

Burt, William, and Grossenheider, Richard. *A Field Guide to the Mammals*. Boston: Houghton-Mifflin Company, 1964

Cahalane, Victor H. *Mammals of North America*. New York: The Macmillan Company, 1947

Hamilton, William J. *The Mammals of Eastern United States*. New York: Hafner Publishing Company, 1943

Ingles, Lloyd G. *Mammals of the Pacific States*. Stanford: Stanford University Press, 1965

Mason, George F. *Animal Tracks*. New York: Morrow & Company, 1943

Murie, Olaus. *A Field Guide to Animal Tracks*. Boston: Houghton-Mifflin Company, 1954

Palmer, E. L. *Palmer's Fieldbook of Mammals*. New York: E. P. Dutton & Company, 1957

GENERAL

Berrill, Jacquelyn. *Wonders of Animal Migration*. New York: Dodd, Mead & Company, 1964

Blond, Georges. *The Great Migrations of Animals*. New York: The Macmillan Company, 1956

Collins, Henry Hill. *Complete Guide to American Wildlife: East, Central, and North*. New York: Harper & Row, Publishers, 1959

May, Charles Paul. *When Animals Change Clothes*. New York: Holiday House, 1965

Morgan, Ann. *Field Book of Animals in Winter*. New York: G. P. Putnam's Sons, 1939

Palmer, E. Laurence. *Fieldbook of Natural History*. New York: McGraw-Hill Book Company, 1949

Sutton, Ann and Myron. *Animals on the Move*. Chicago: Rand McNally & Company, 1962

MAGAZINES

National Wildlife, published by National Wildlife Federation, Washington, D. C.

Audubon Magazine, published by National Audubon Society, New York, N. Y.

National History (Incorporating *Nature Magazine*), published by American Museum of Natural History, New York, N. Y.

National Geographic Magazine, published by National Geographic Society, Washington, D. C.

Nature and Science, published by American Museum of Natural History, New York, N. Y.